Thelwell's Sporting Prints

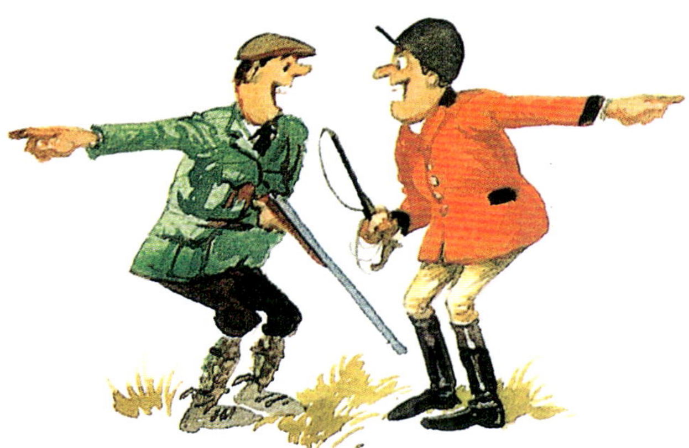

by Norman Thelwell

Angels on Horseback *Thelwell Country*
Thelwell's Riding Academy *The Compleat Tangler*
A Leg at Each Corner *The Effluent Society*
Top Dog *Belt Up*
Thelwell's Book of Leisure *Thelwell Goes West*
Penelope *Thelwell's Gymkhana*
This Desirable Plot *Thelwell's Magnificat*
Penelope Rides Again

Thelwell's Pony Cavalcade
(containing *A Leg at Each Corner*
Thelwell's Riding Academy and
Angels on Horseback)

Thelwell's Pony Panorama
(containing *Gymkhana*,
Thelwell Goes West and *Penelope*)

· THELWELL'S SPORTING PRINTS ·

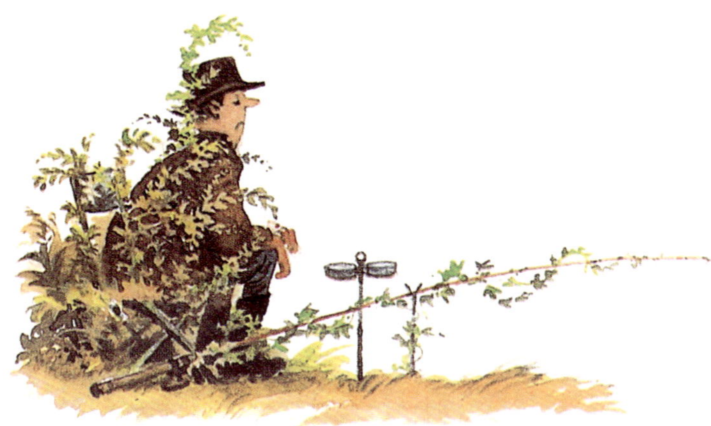

A Methuen Paperback

A Methuen Paperback

First published in Great Britain 1984
This paperback edition published 2008 by
Methuen, 8 Artillery Row, London SW1P 1RZ

A CIP catalogue record for this book
is available from the British Library

ISBN 978 0 413 61900 6

Printed in Great Britain
By Newgate Concise

Contents

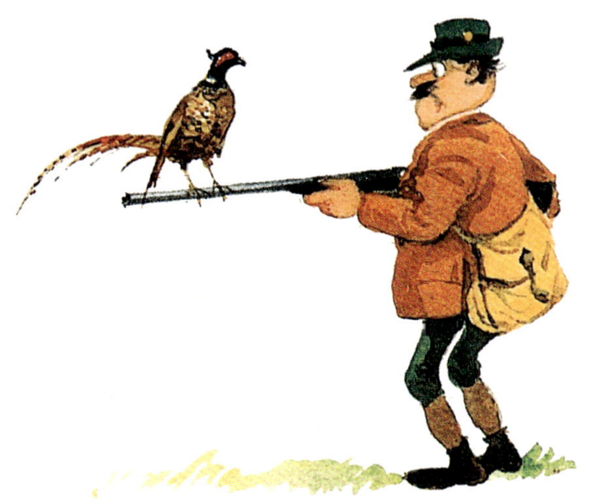

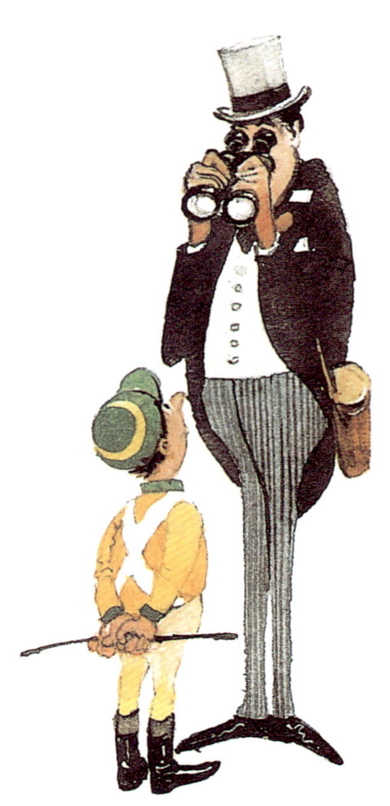

Foreword

What a privilege it is to contribute a foreword to Norman Thelwell's *Sporting Prints*. Not only is the name of Thelwell associated all over the world with a very special kind of humour—particularly, perhaps, for those who have ever had any sort of connection with ponies—but it is true to say that his name has become part of our vocabulary. People talk about a thelwell pony, and everybody knows exactly what they are talking about, in just the same way as people know what you mean if you refer to a bowdlerism or a malapropism. That surely is fame indeed.

But in the case of Norman Thelwell it is fame properly deserved. Over the years he has given an enormous amount of pleasure to people from every walk of life, in his books, on Christmas cards and calendars, pictures and prints, even on teatowels.

It is not easy to analyse his genius, for that he possesses a unique genius no one can deny. In the first place every picture tells a humorous story or anecdote, one with which almost everyone can identify, especially if they have been involved in any of the sports that he depicts.

Secondly, there is so often in his pictures an element of basic truth. It is not just that we recognise a situation—a child being bucked off, a horse running away, a shot hitting the wrong target, but we know that behind the picture, despite the fact that it is a caricature, lies a truism: these mishaps are experienced by ordinary people, because such is the nature of human beings.

The third reason for the popularity of Thelwell is that although there is an immediate, general impression of what the artist is, in his own inimitable style, portraying, there is too a wealth of detail: branches, clouds, details of dress and accessories—they are all there, which, in fact, is something that appeals very much to people. While obviously there is a real appreciation of impressionistic or abstract work, yet most people, I believe, enjoy detail. 'It makes it so real,' one hears people say; partly, perhaps, again because they recognise things with which they are familiar.

Finally, Norman Thelwell is a real artist with the artist's sense of colour and form and composition. There is never anything slipshod about his work, or amateurish. We are just fortunate in that an artist so talented has directed his ability in a way that has such popular appeal: just as we are fortunate in that one whose real passion in life is fishing has, through experiences with his own children and acquaintances, been able to divert his attention to such a wide range of sports and recreations.

In *Sporting Prints* we get a marvellous selection of his work covering the whole of the 'hunting, shooting, fishing' and racing scene: hilarious, outrageous, but never very far from the truth.

Sporting Prints is going to bring a great many people many happy hours of entertainment.

Dorian Williams

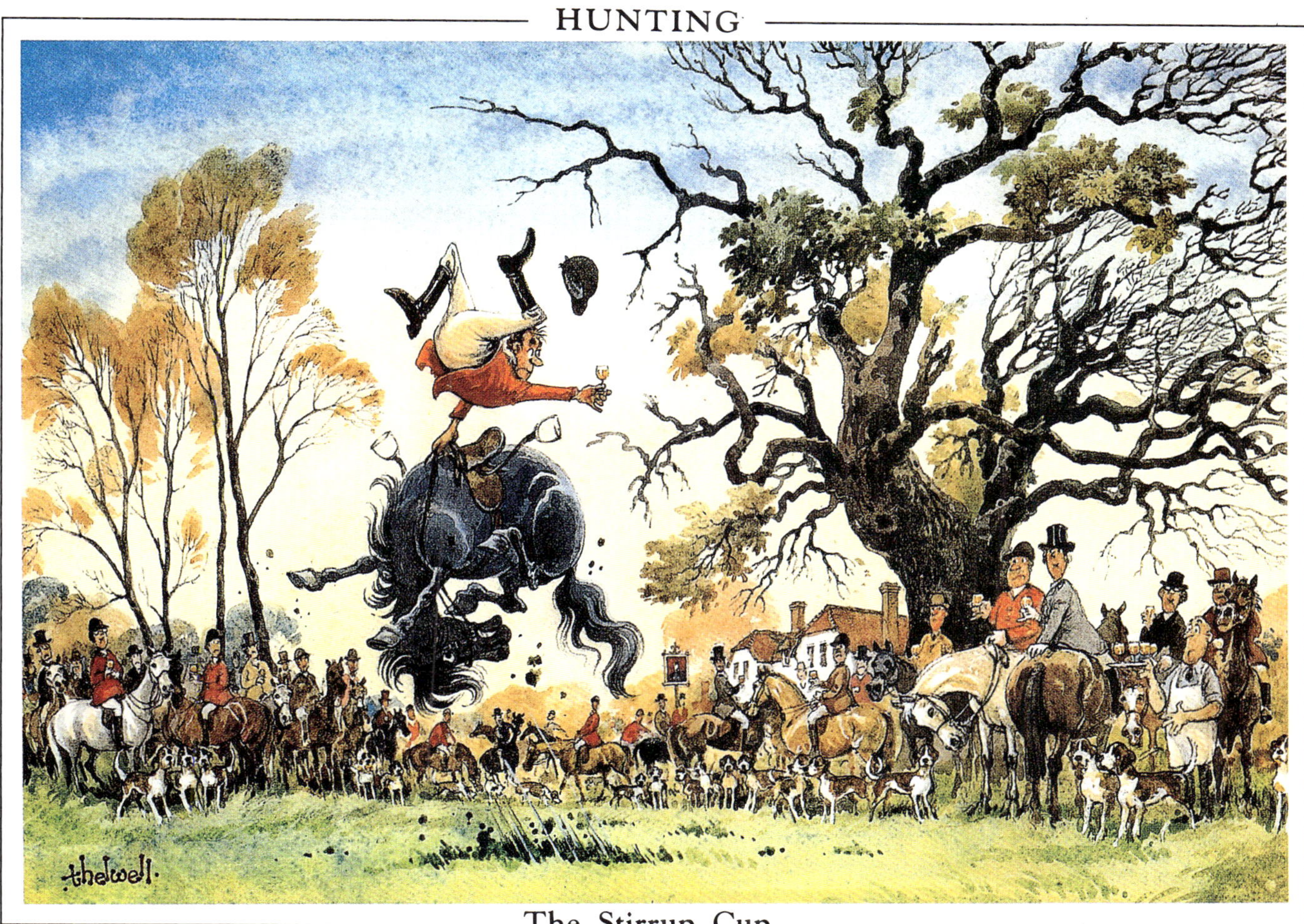

The Stirrup Cup

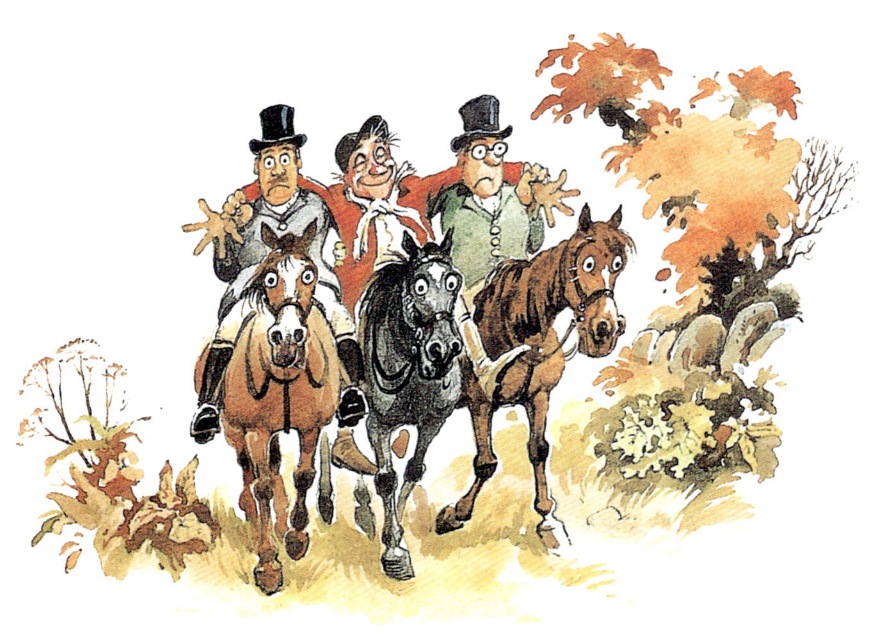

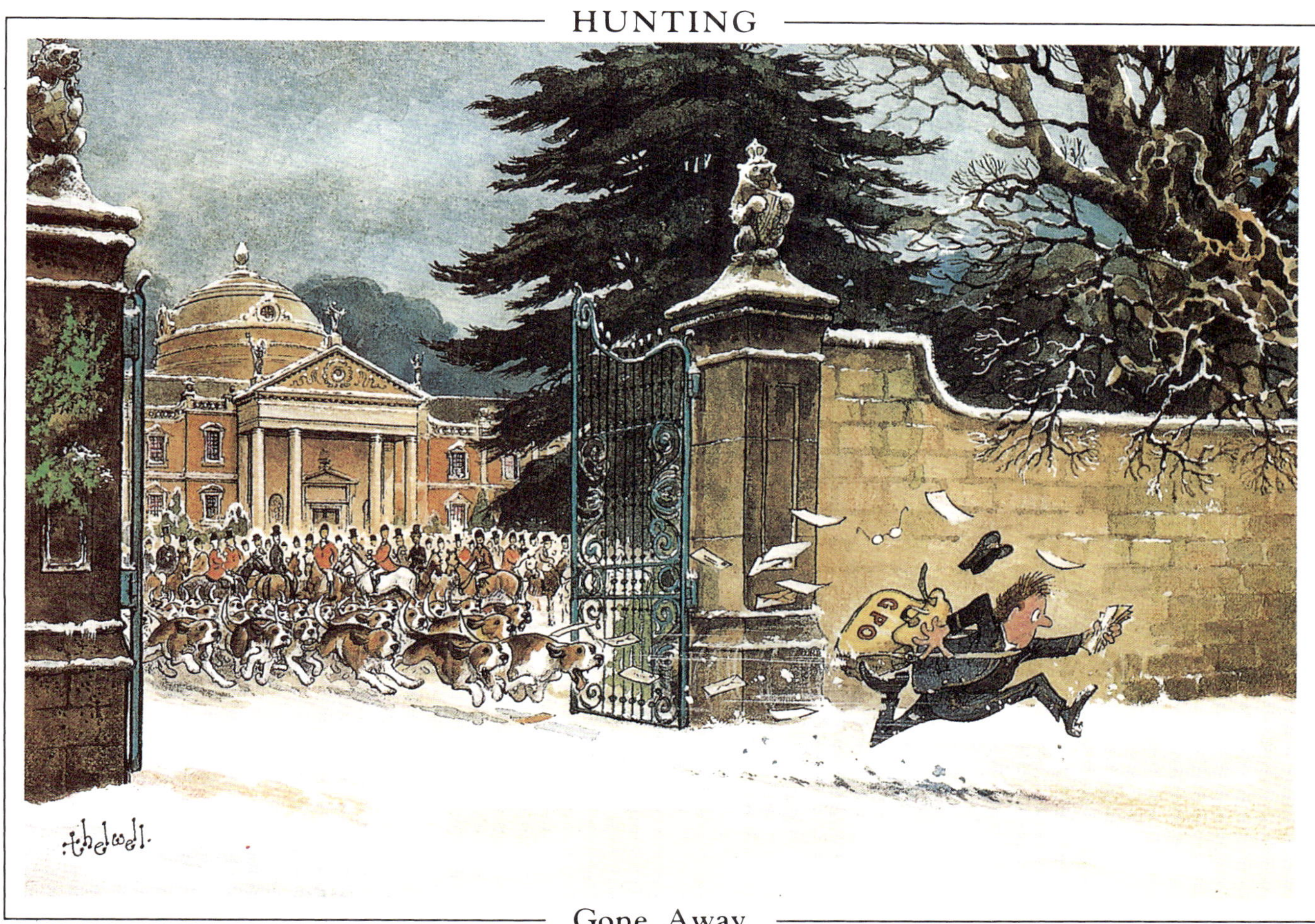

Gone Away

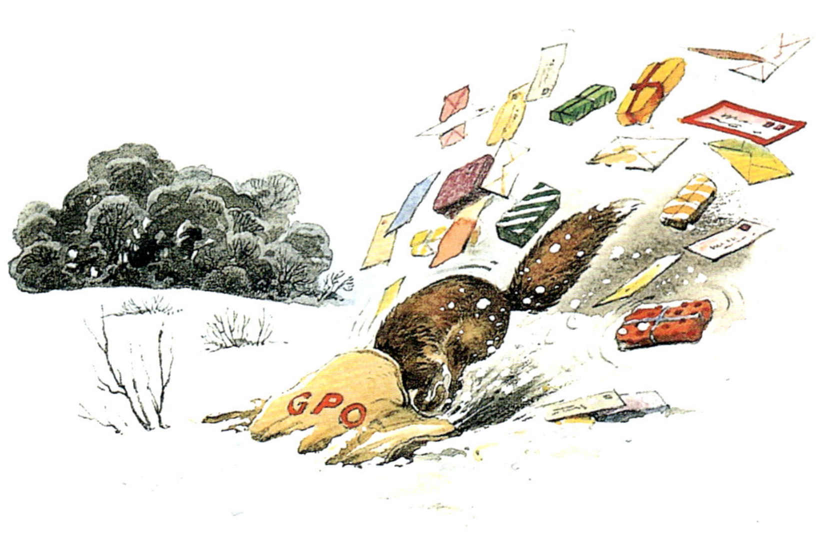

GPO

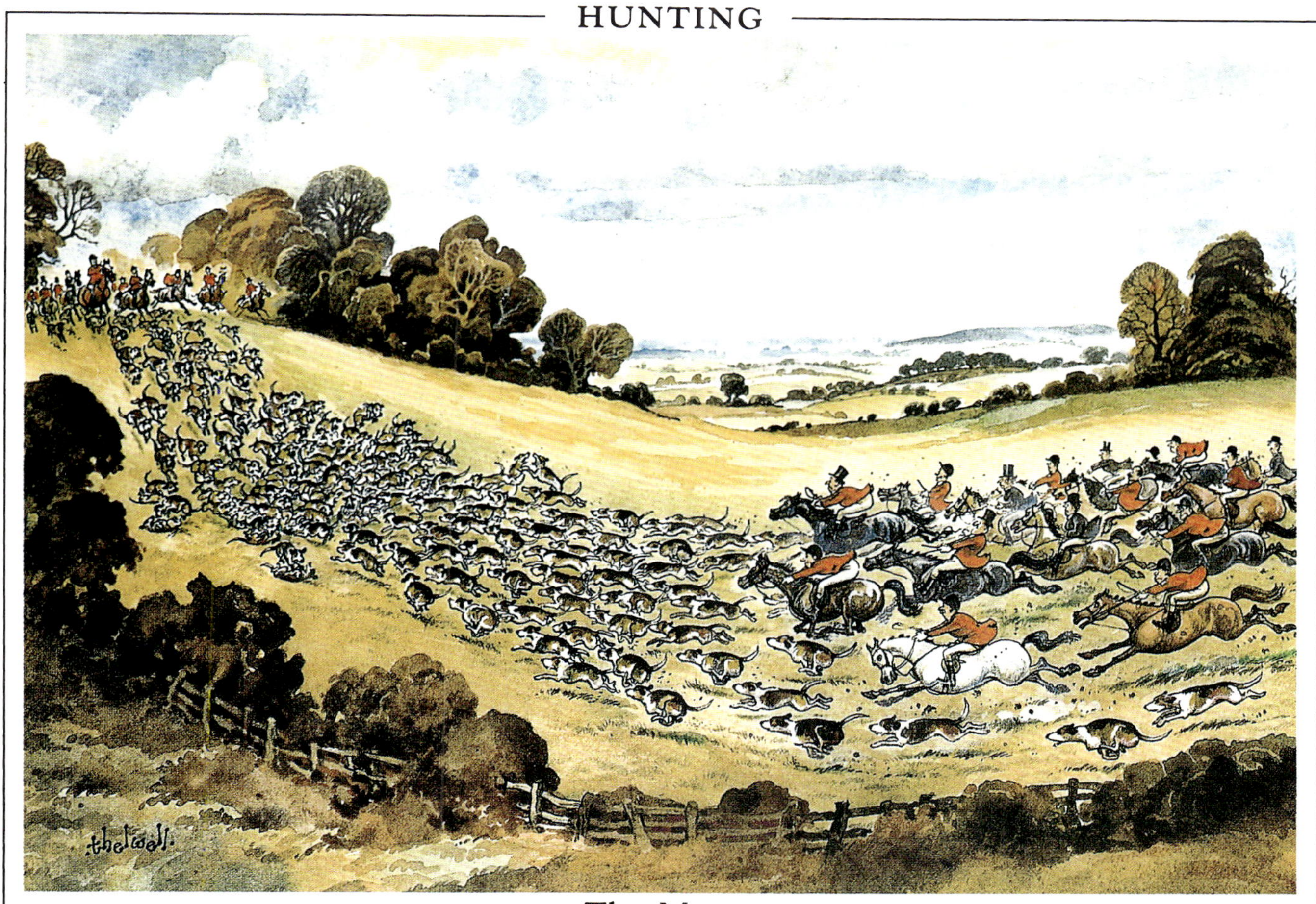

The Meet

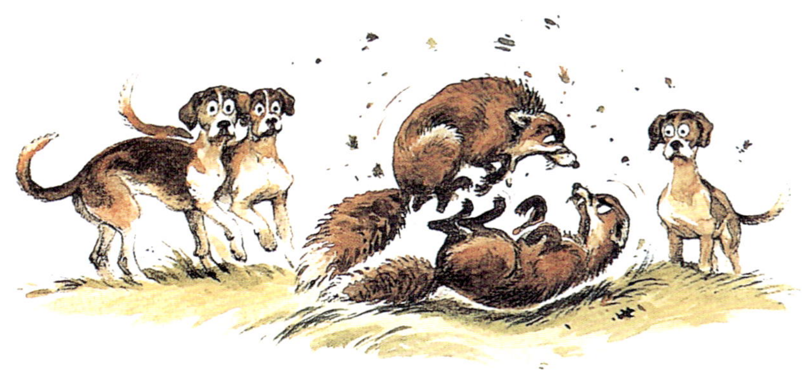

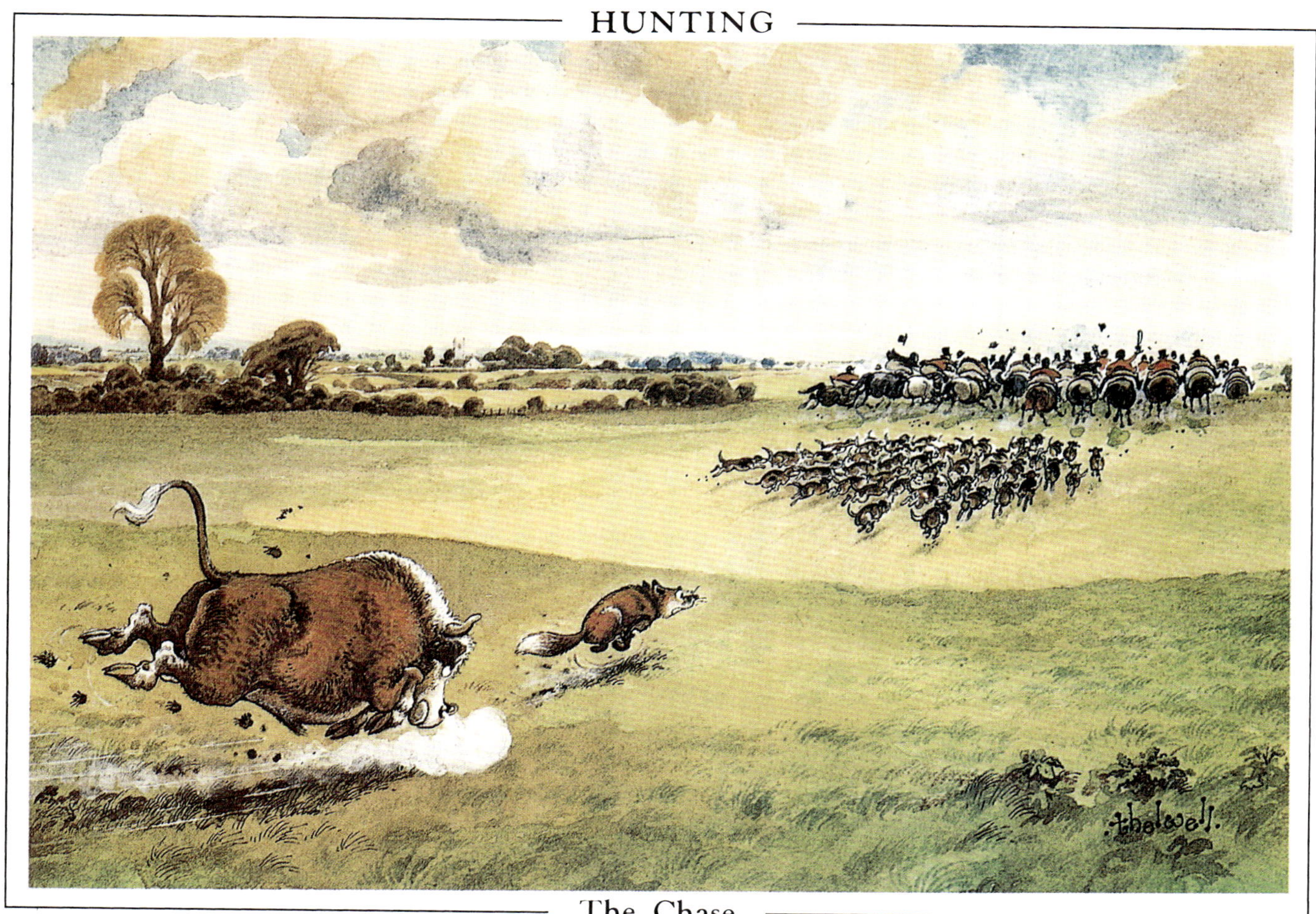

The Chase

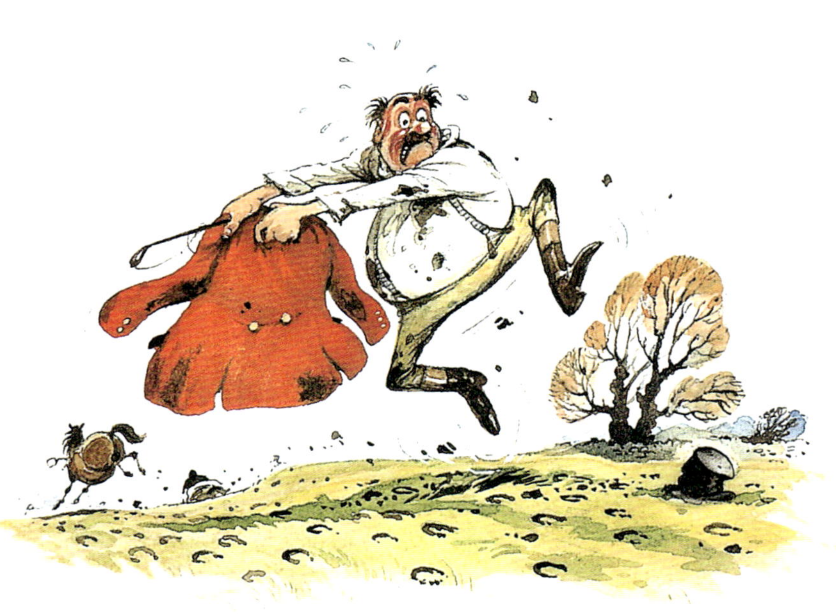

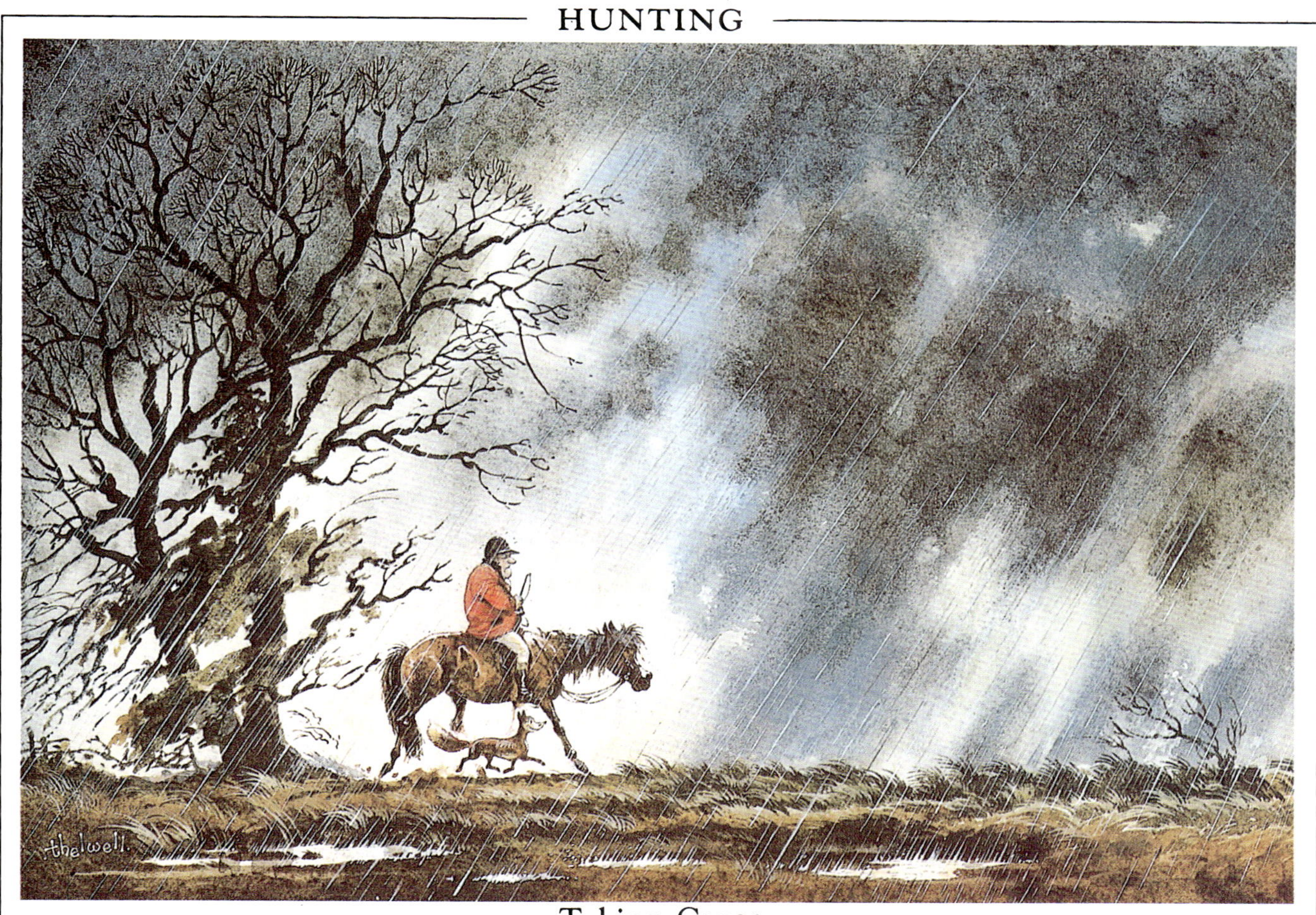

Taking Cover

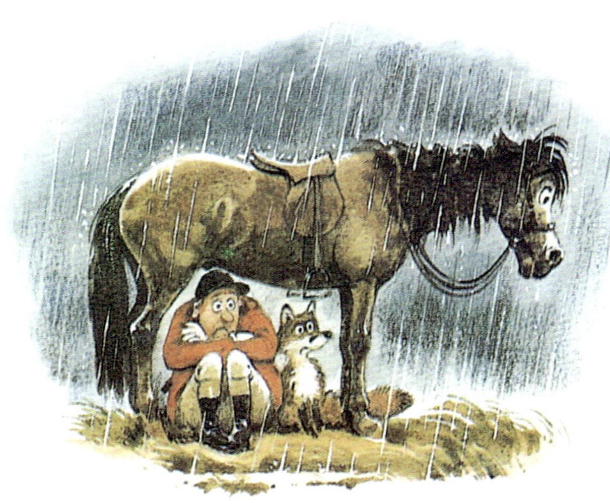

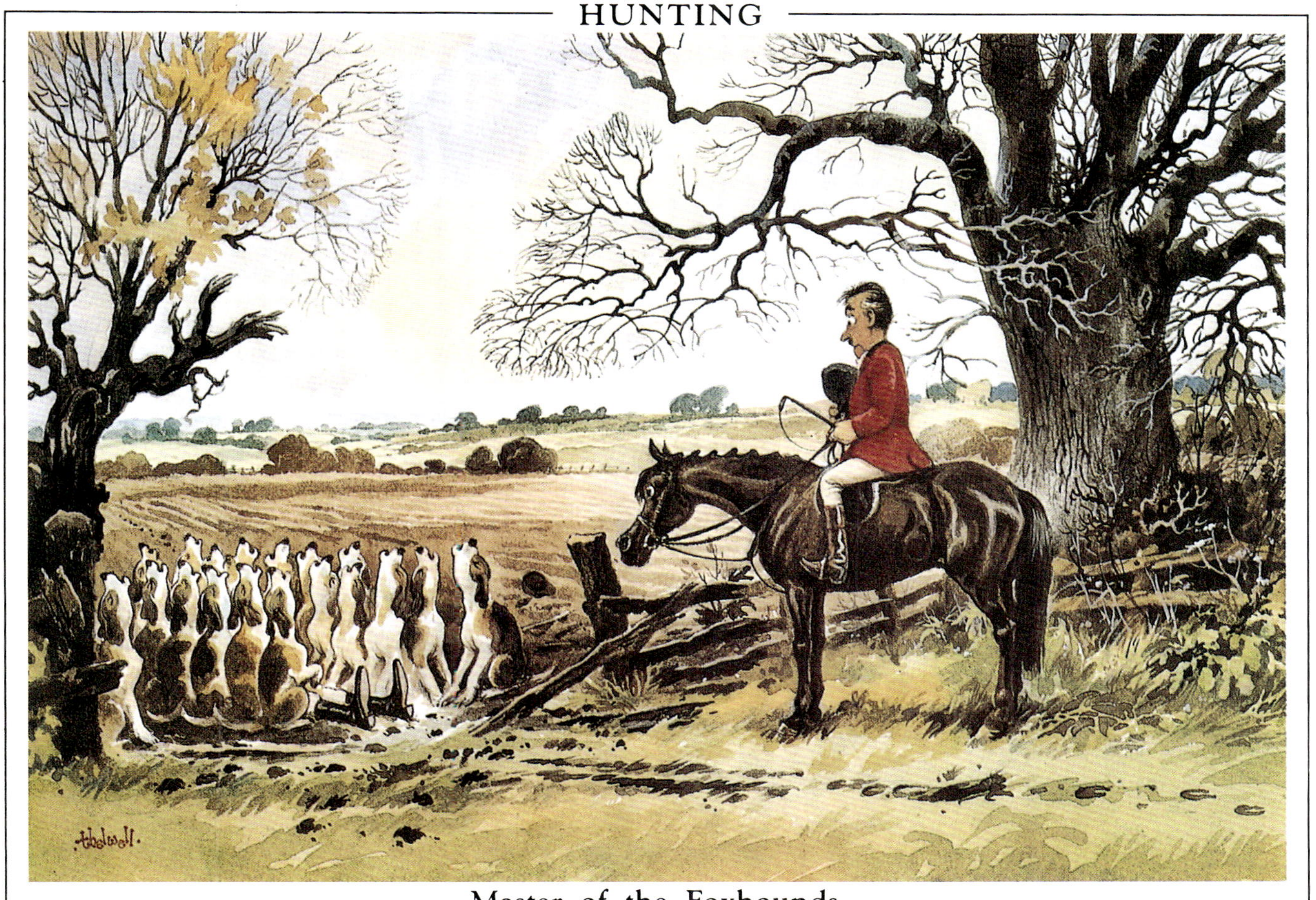

Master of the Foxhounds

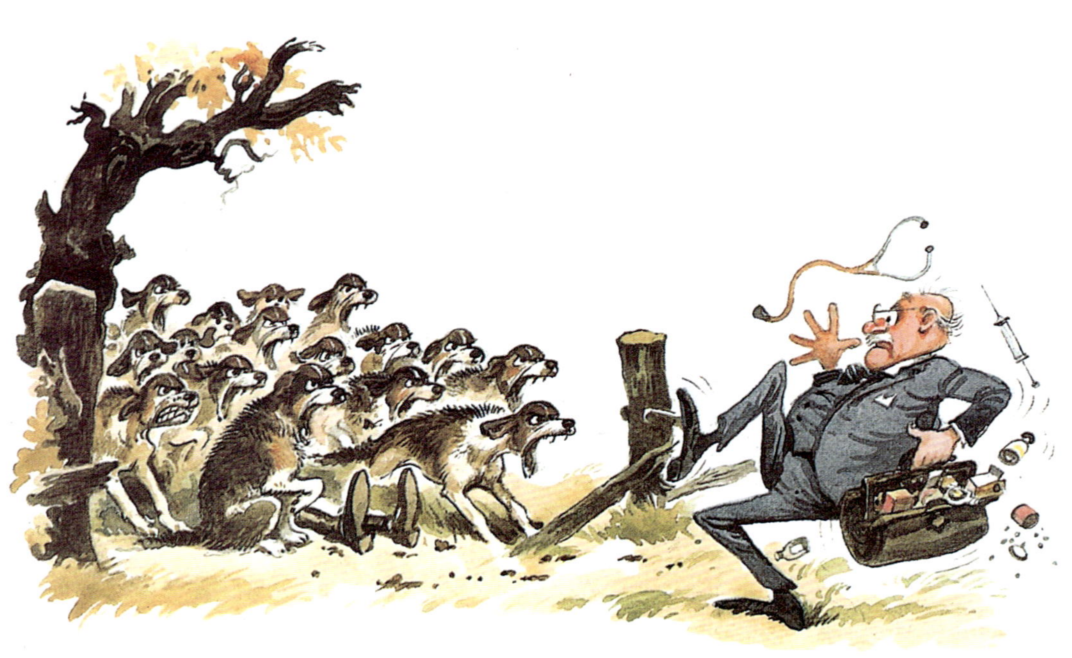

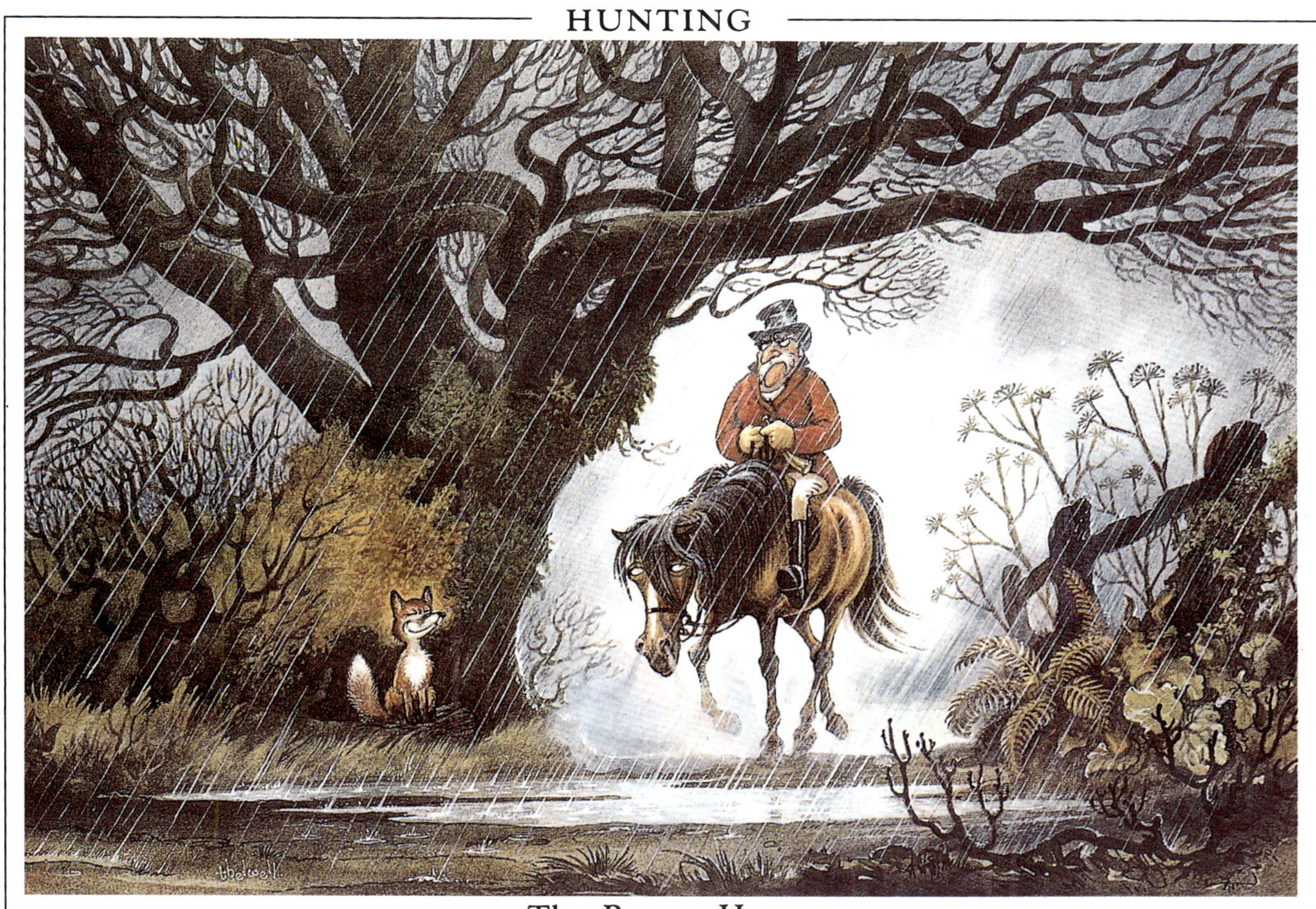

The Return Home

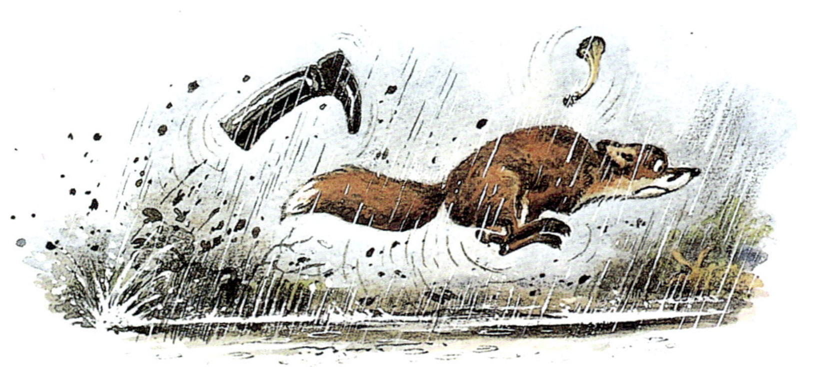

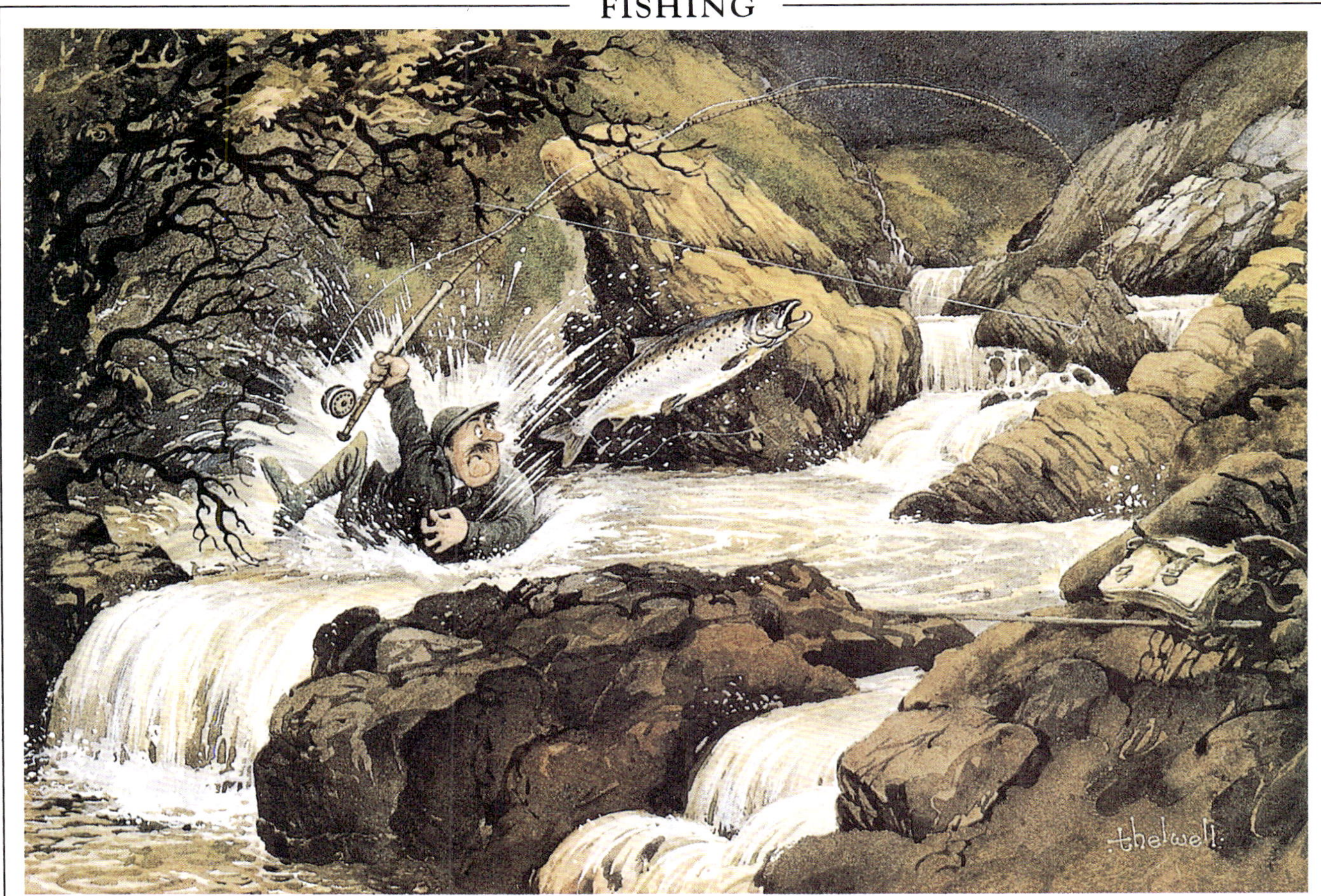

The Game Fisherman

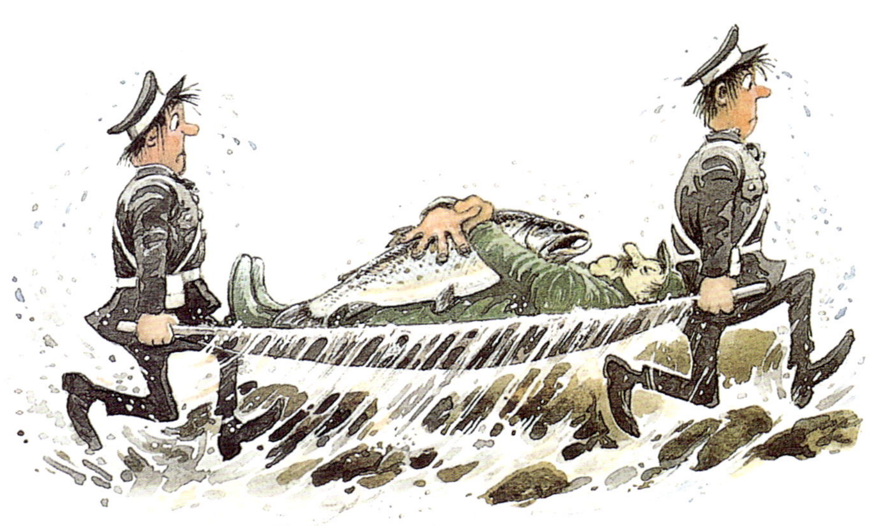

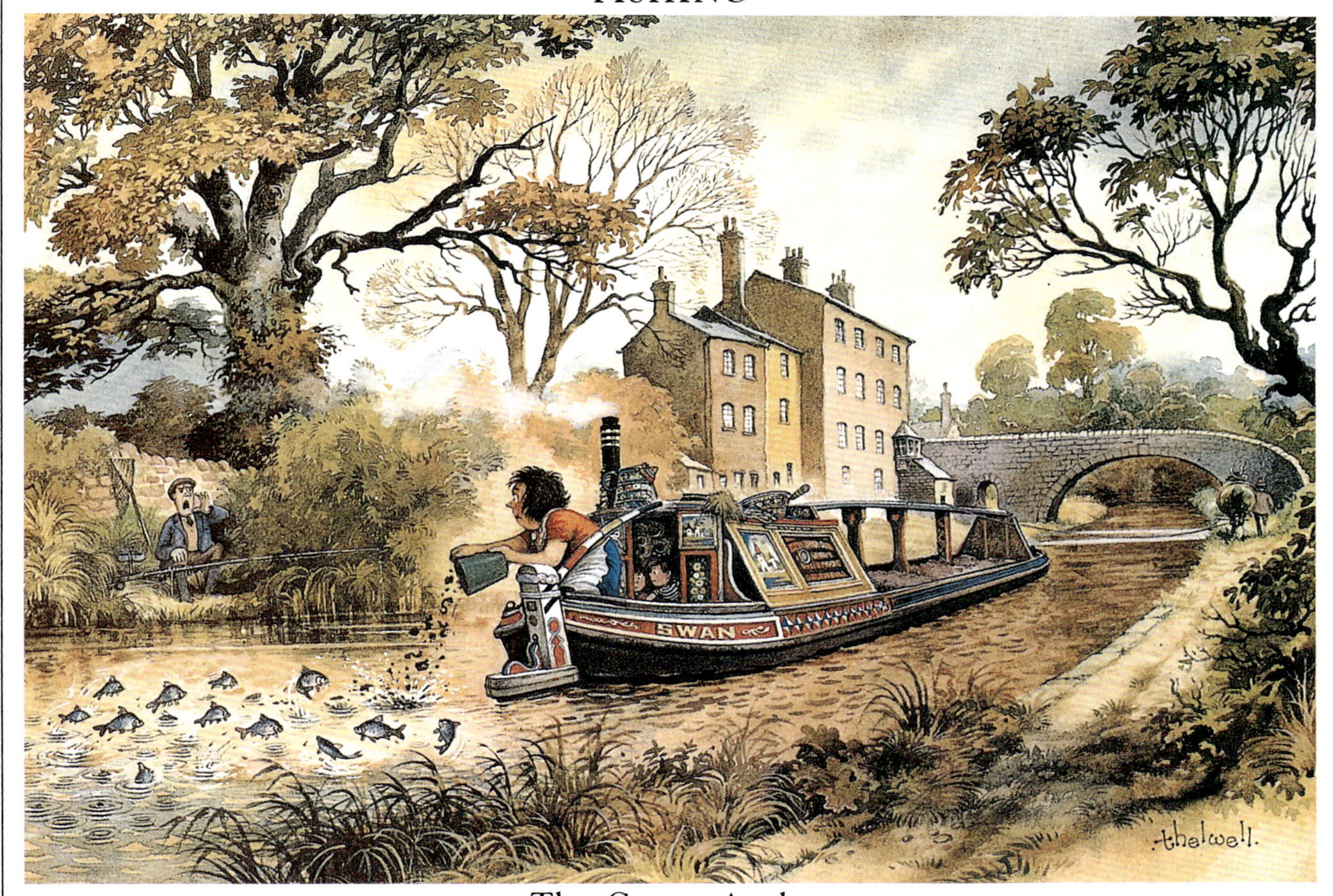

The Coarse Angler

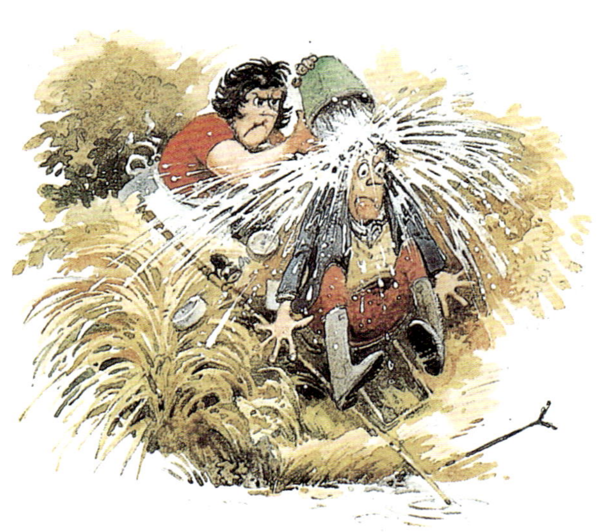

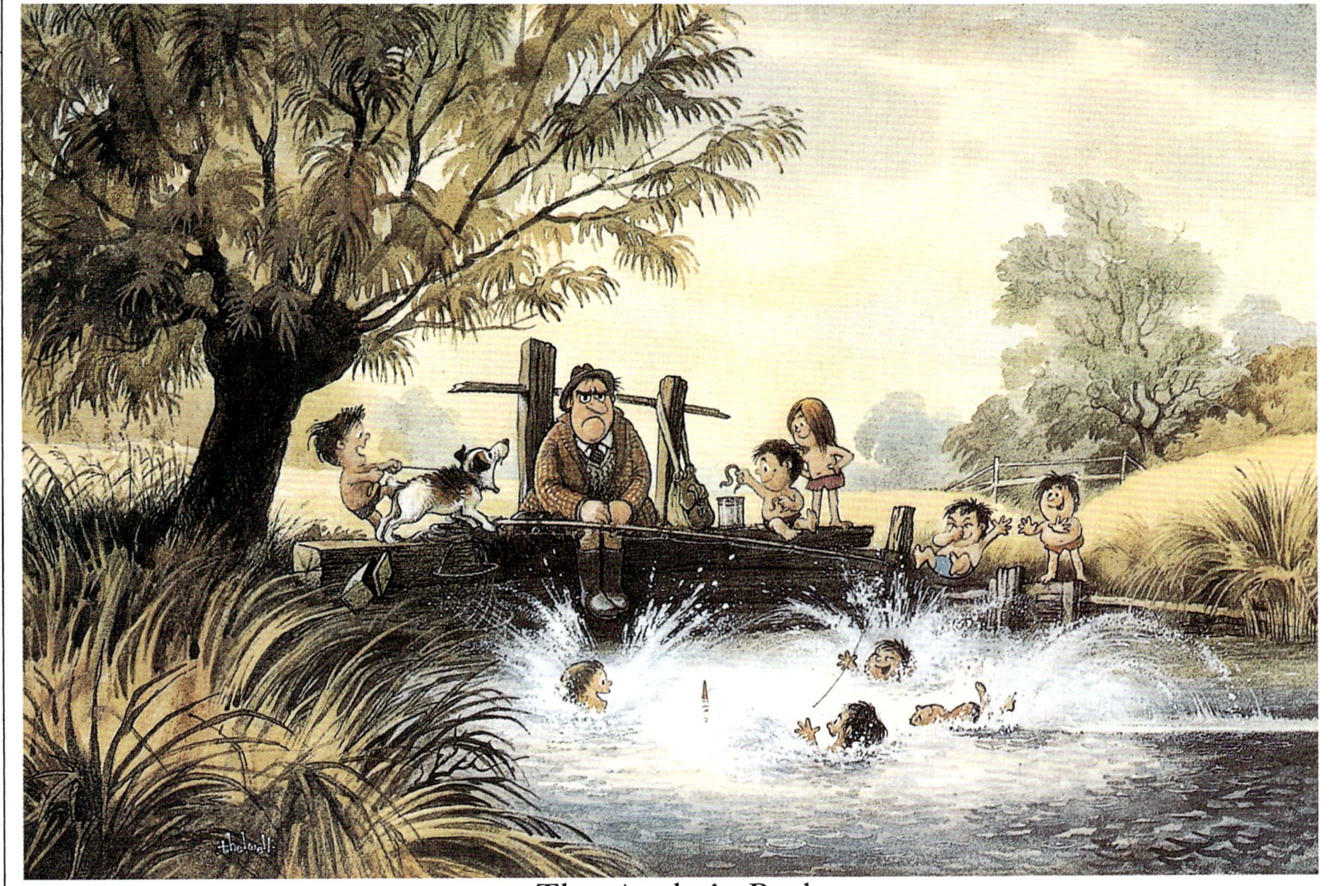

The Angler's Pool

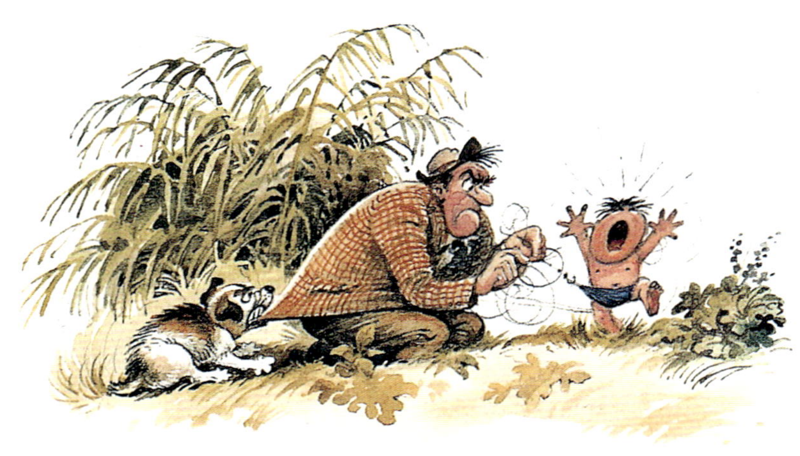

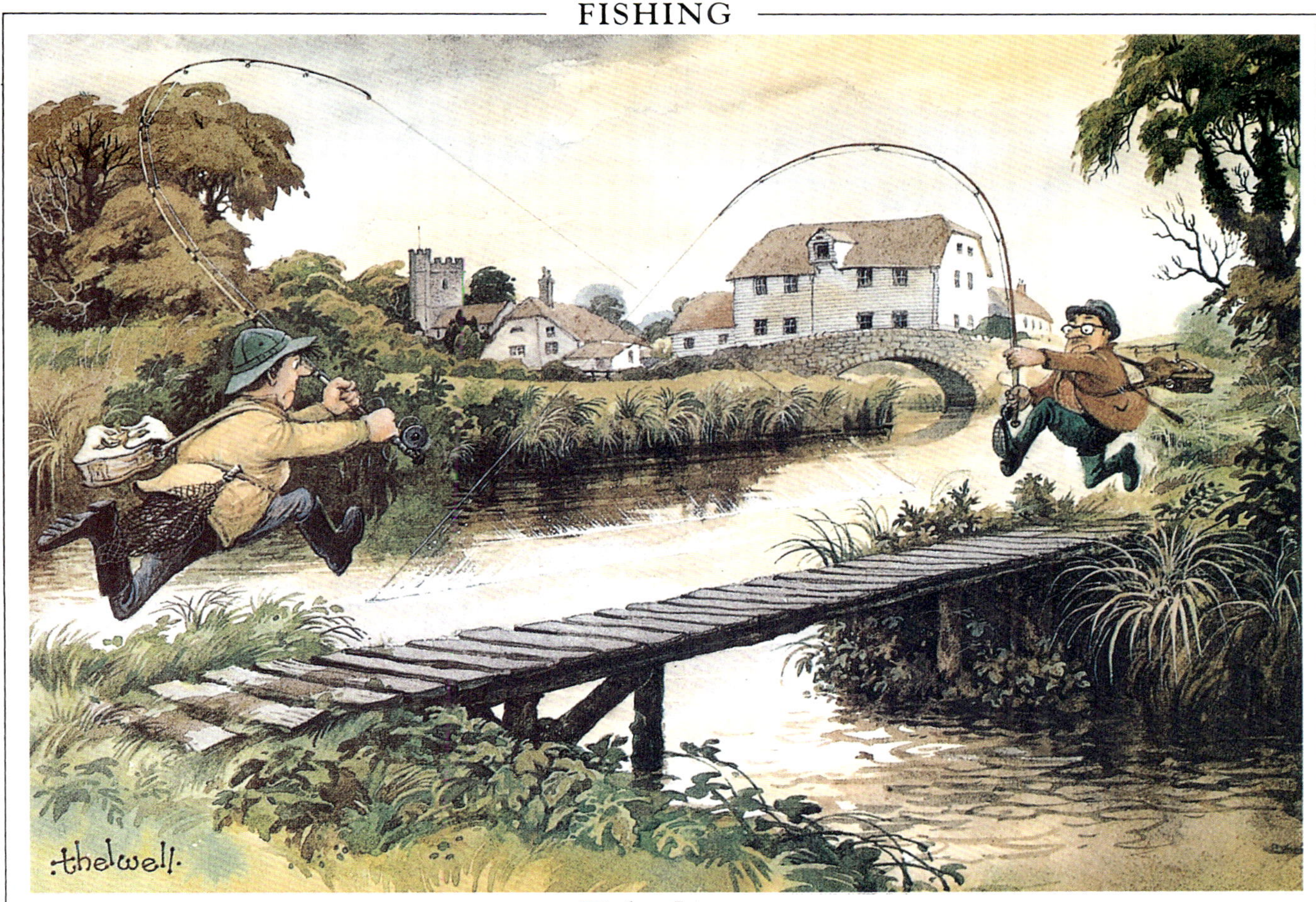

Tight Lines

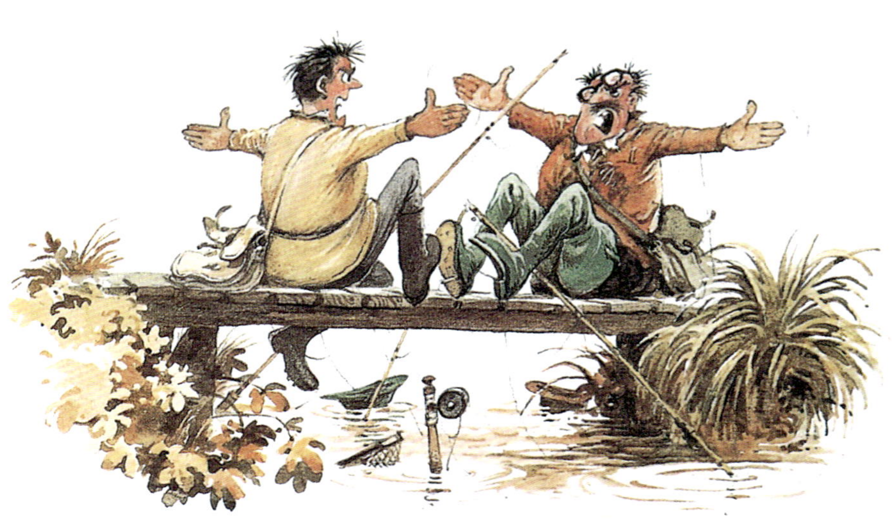

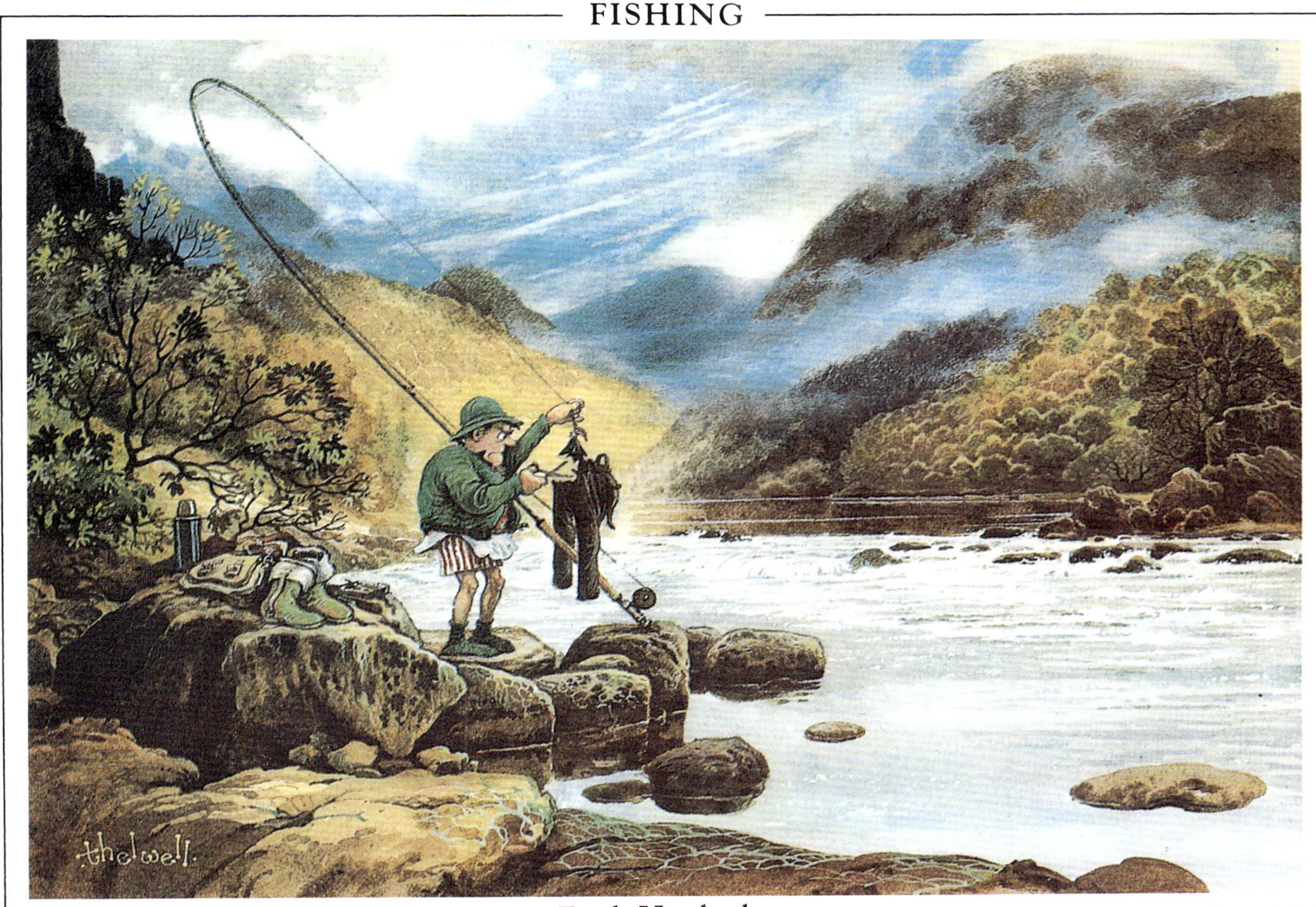

Foul Hooked

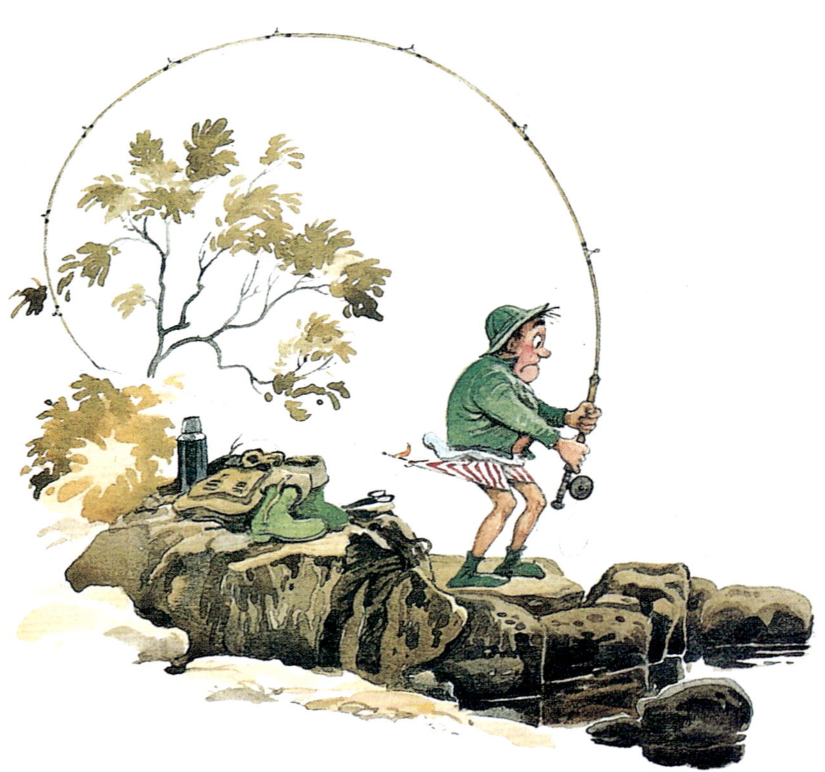

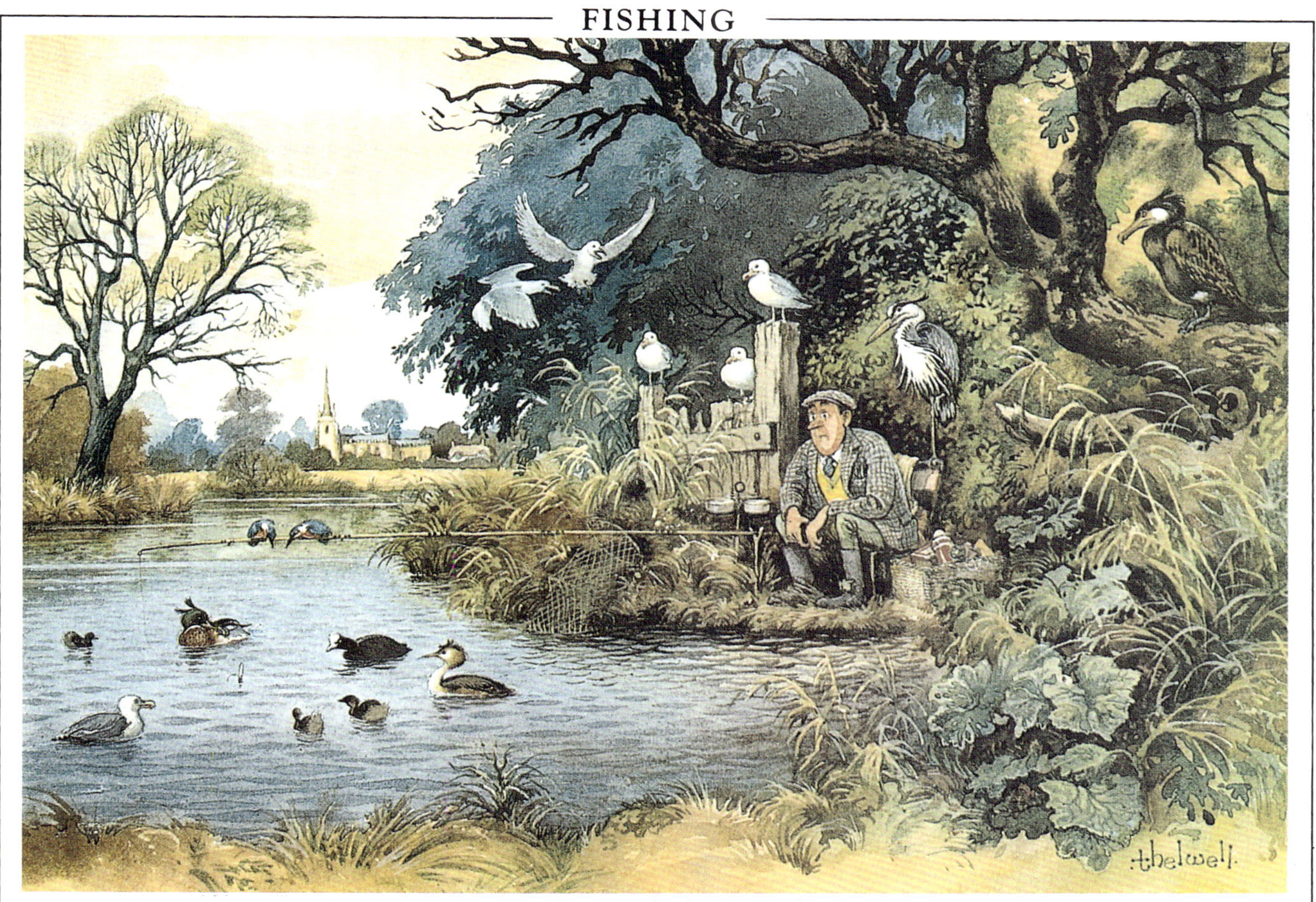

Brothers of the Angle

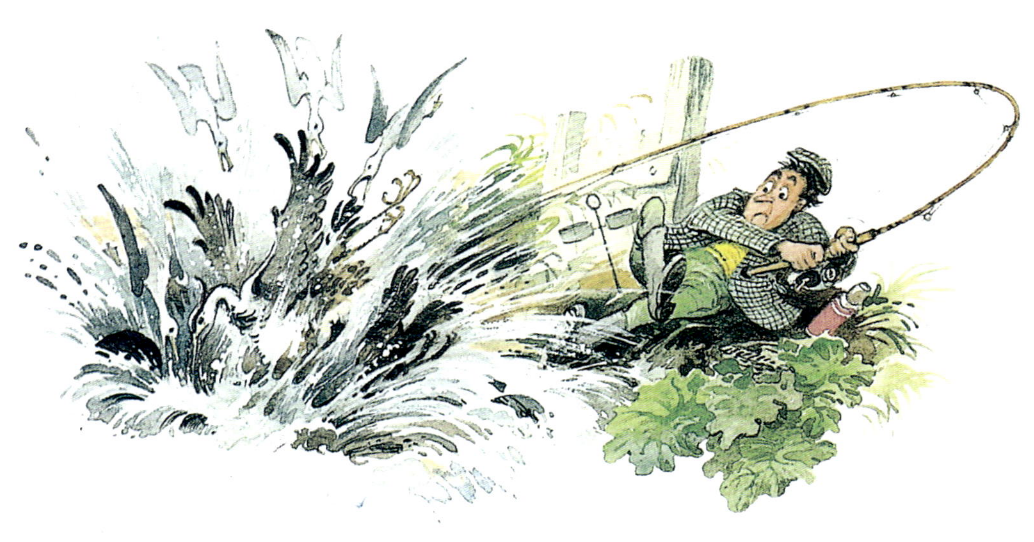

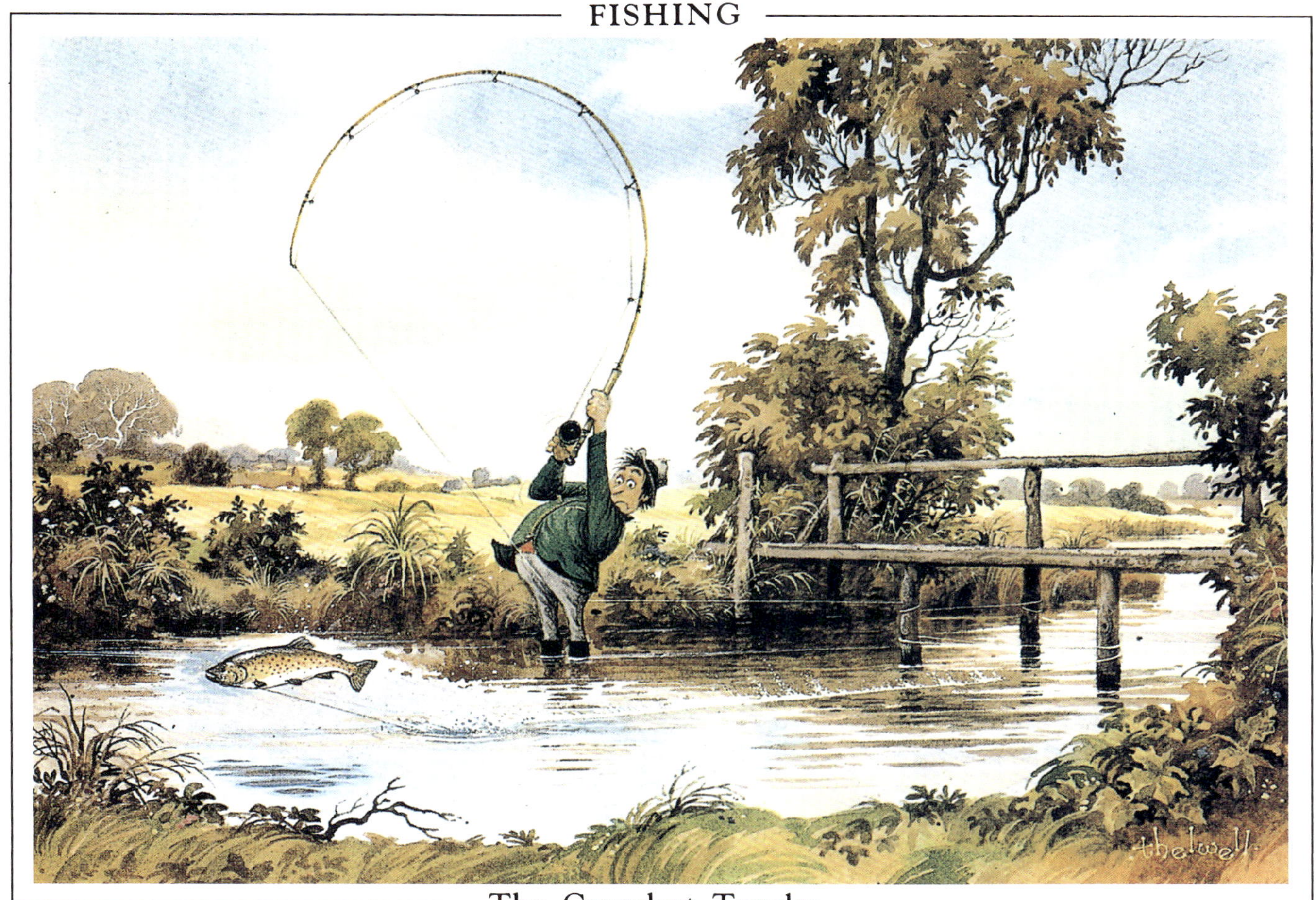

The Compleat Tangler

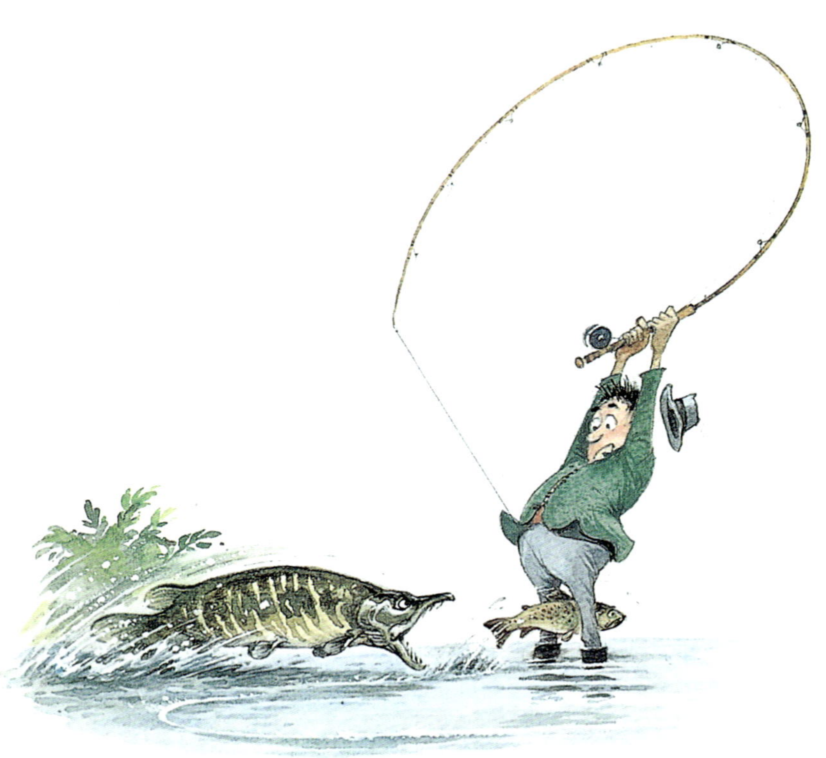

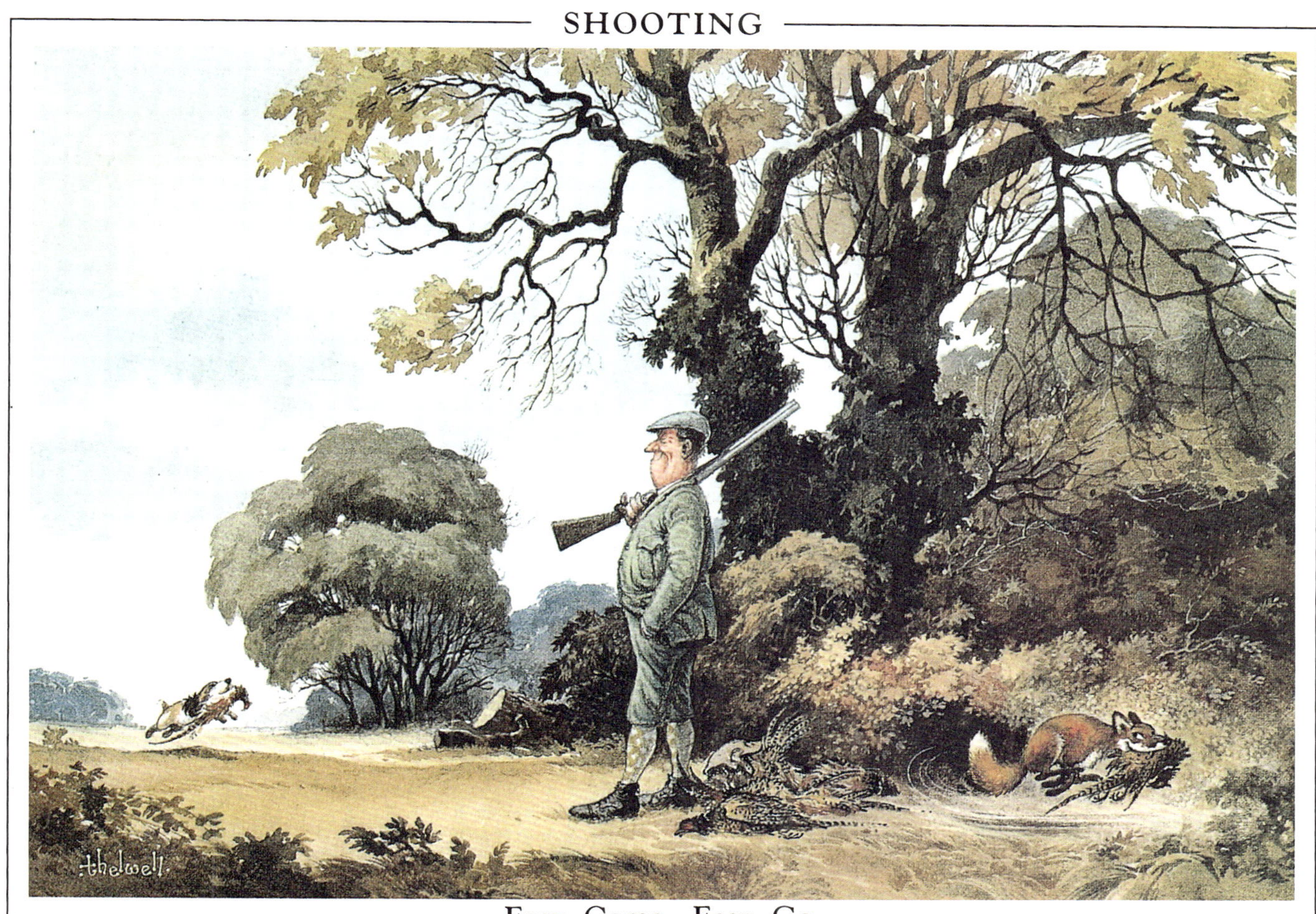

Easy Come—Easy Go

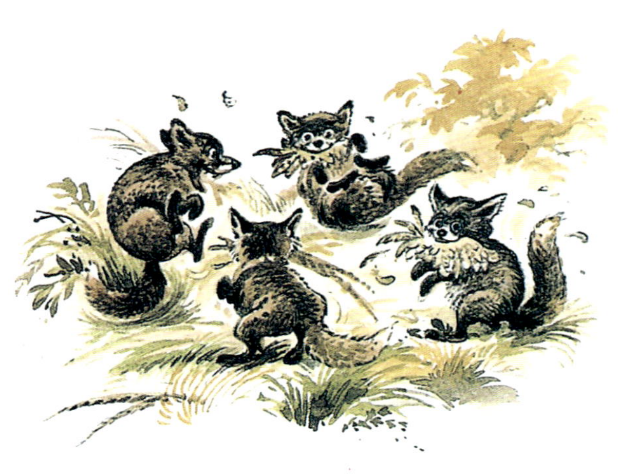

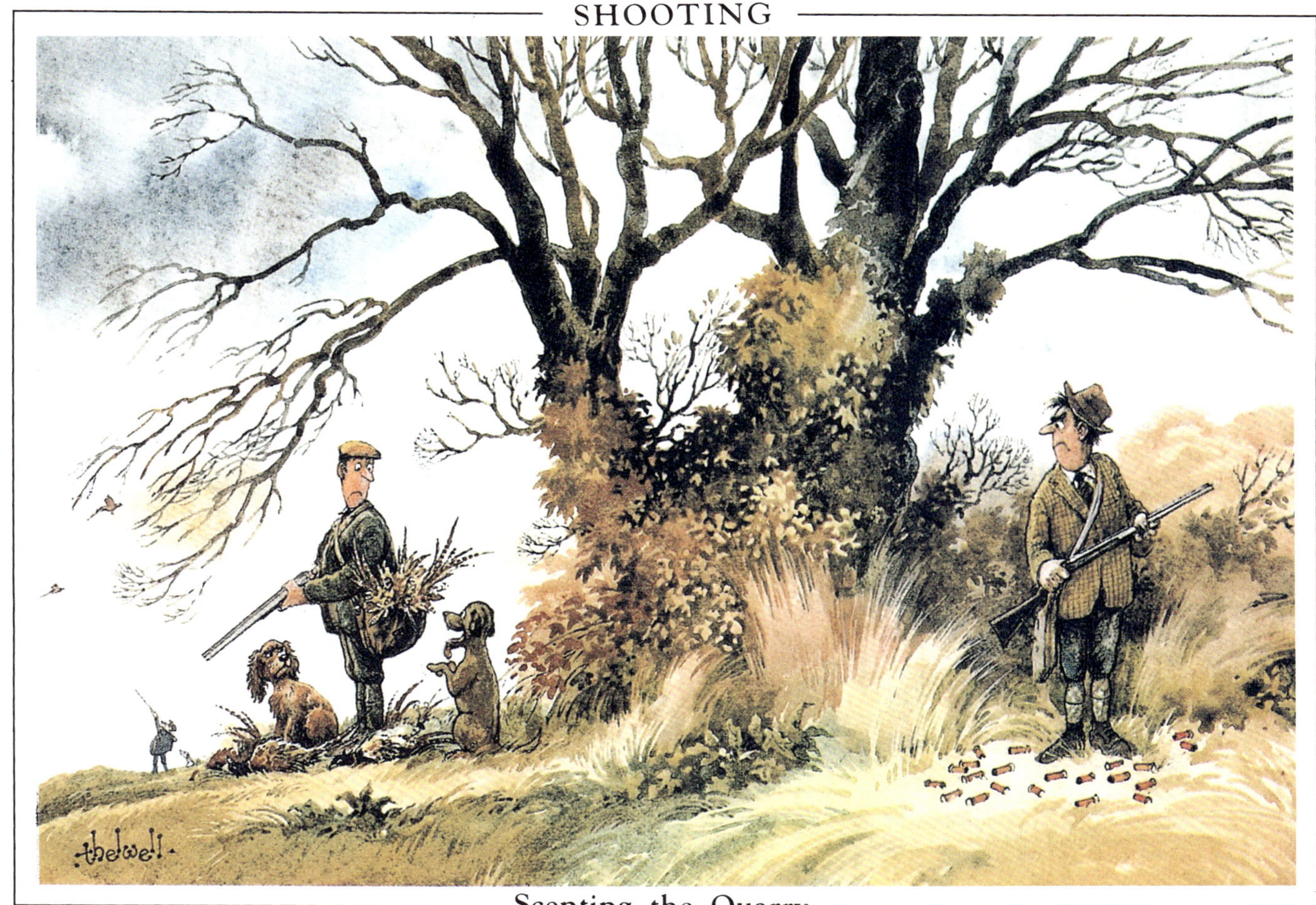

Scenting the Quarry

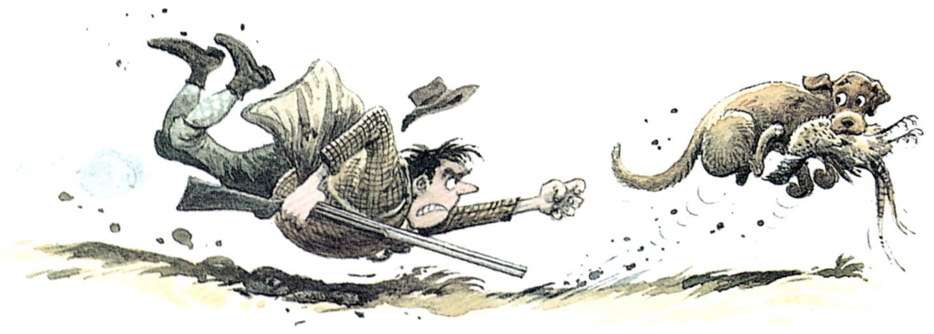

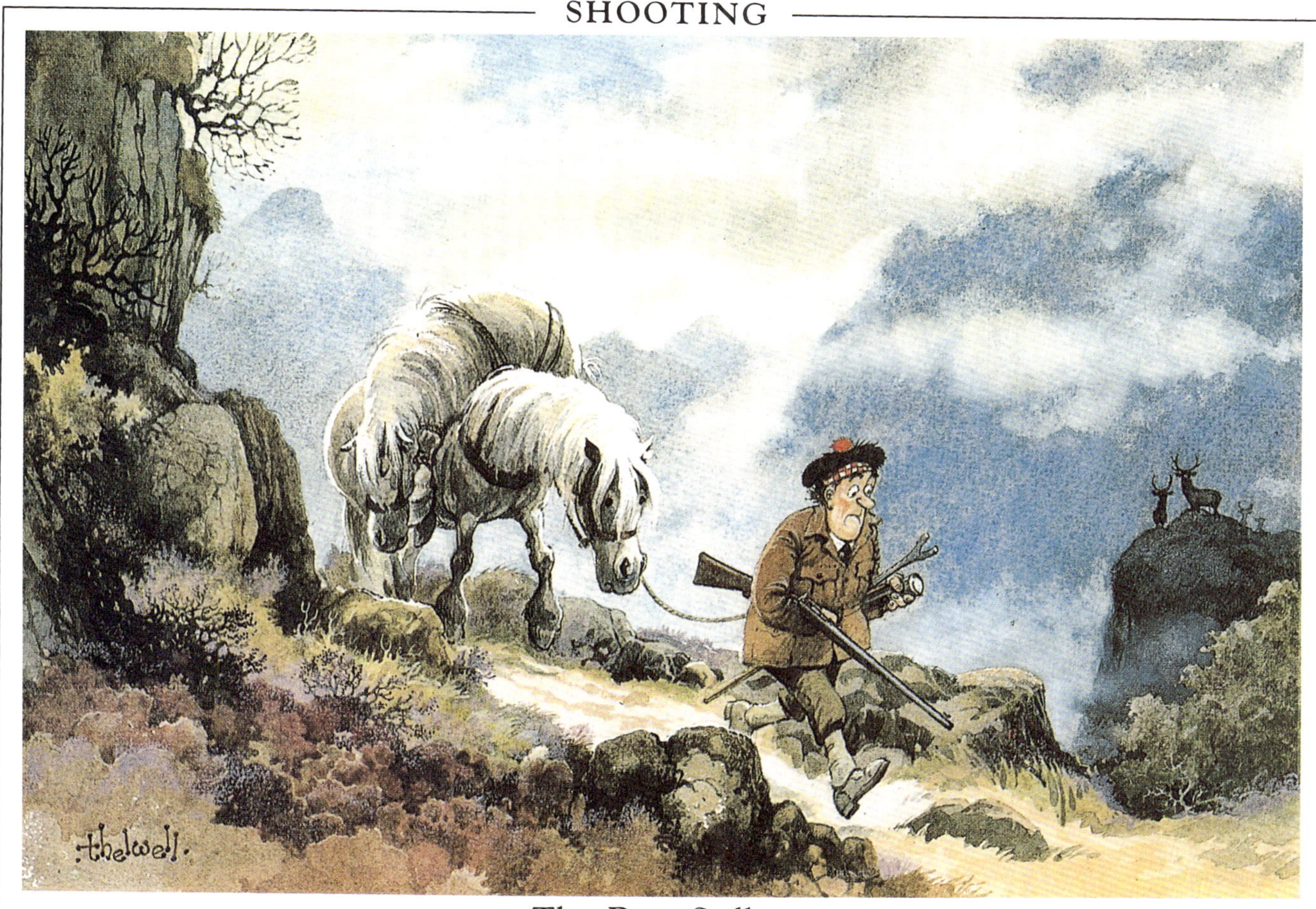

The Deer Stalker

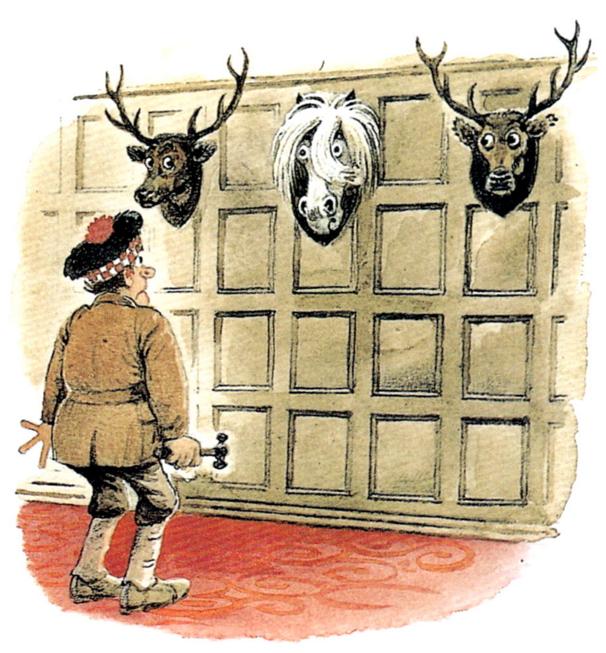

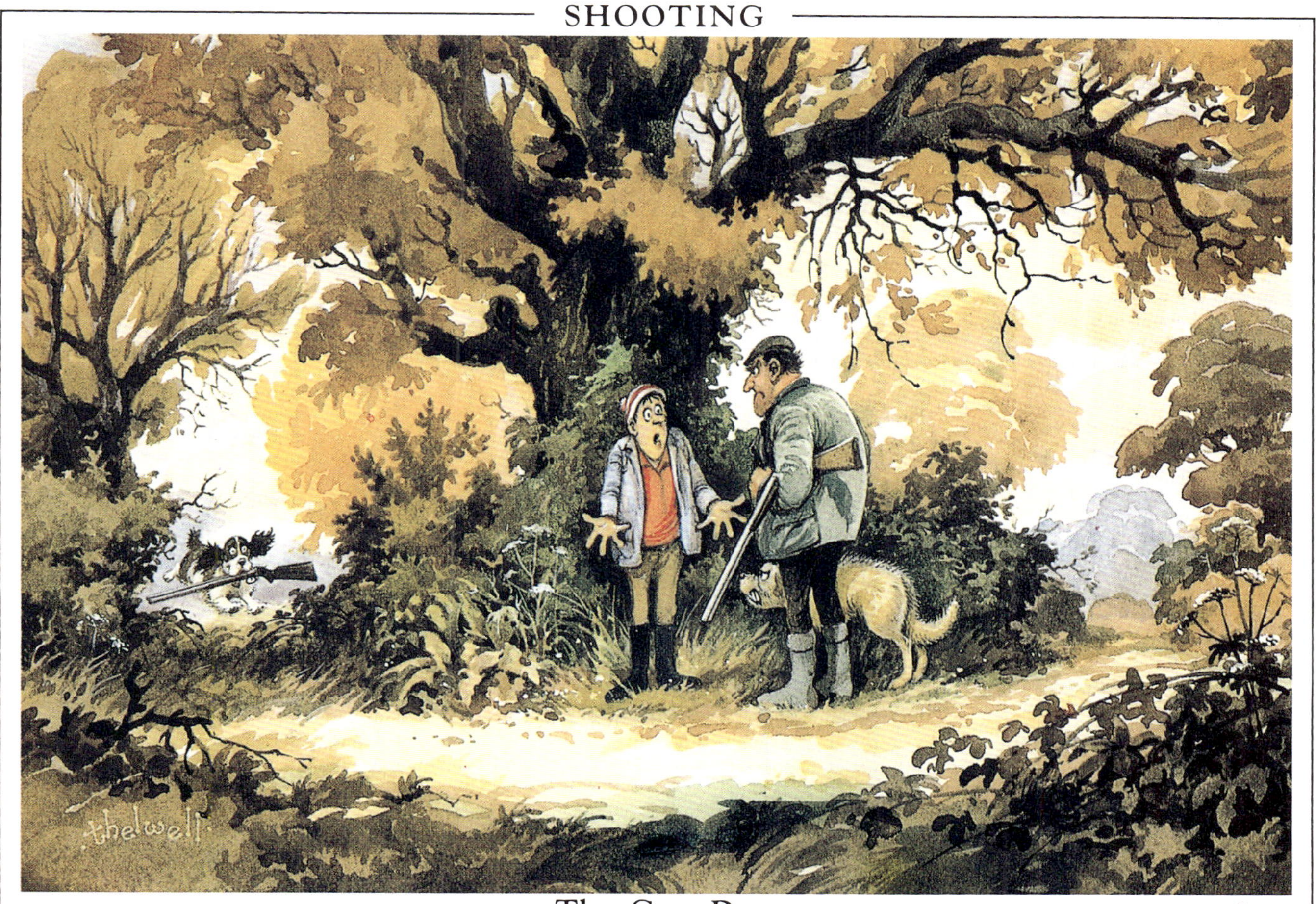

The Gun Dog

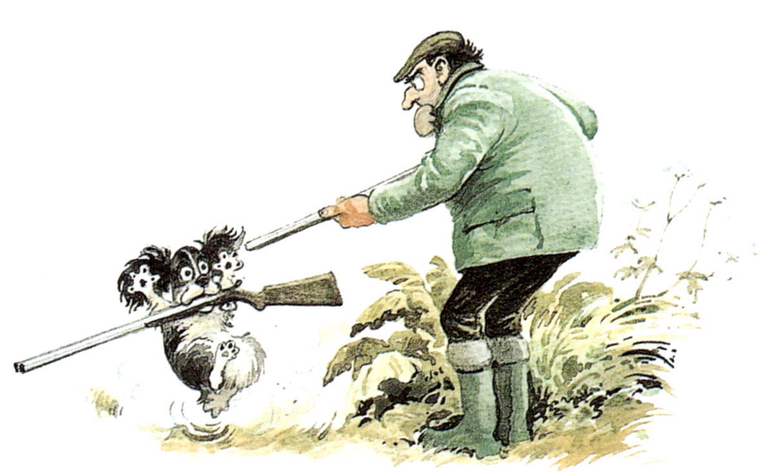

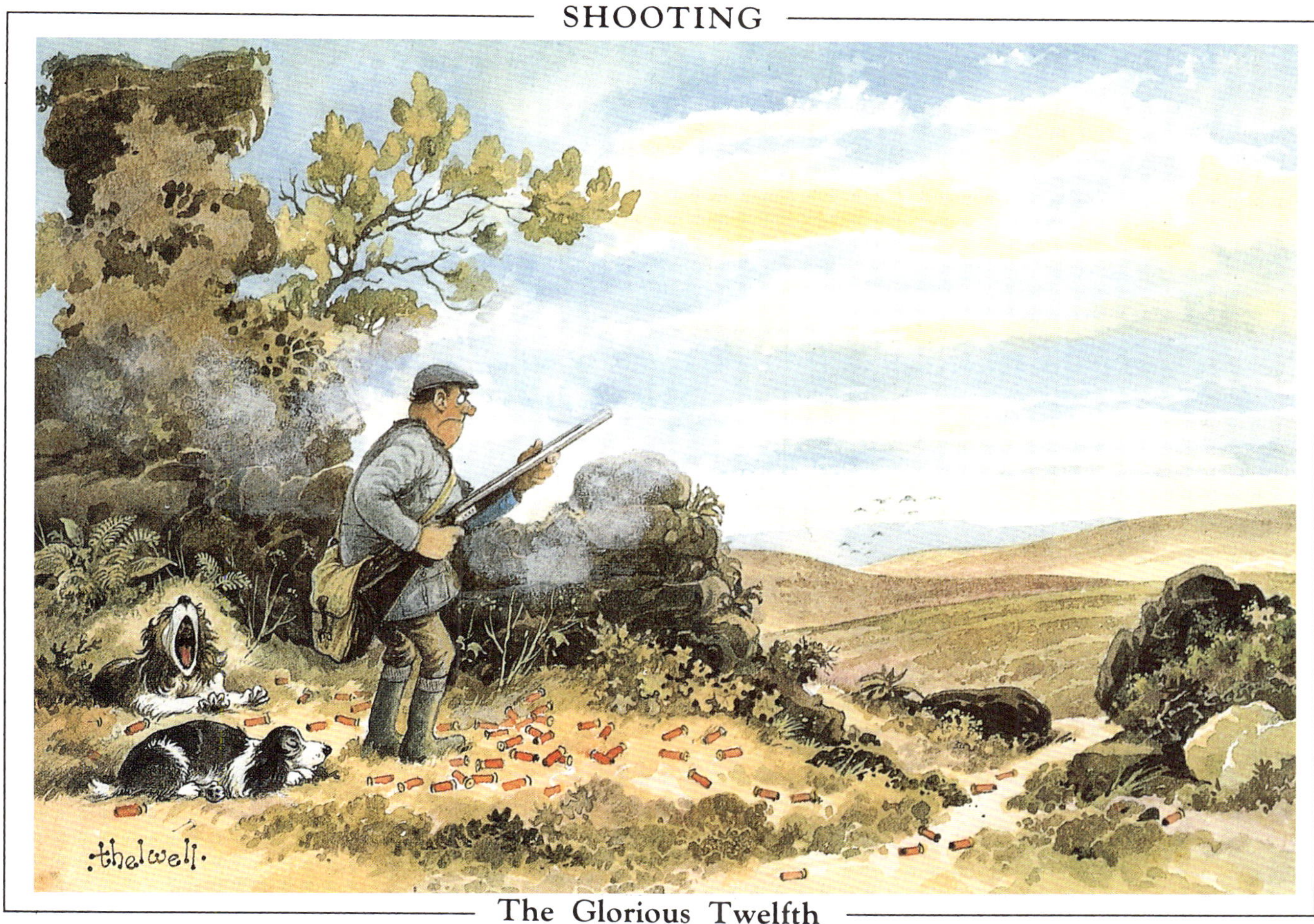

The Glorious Twelfth

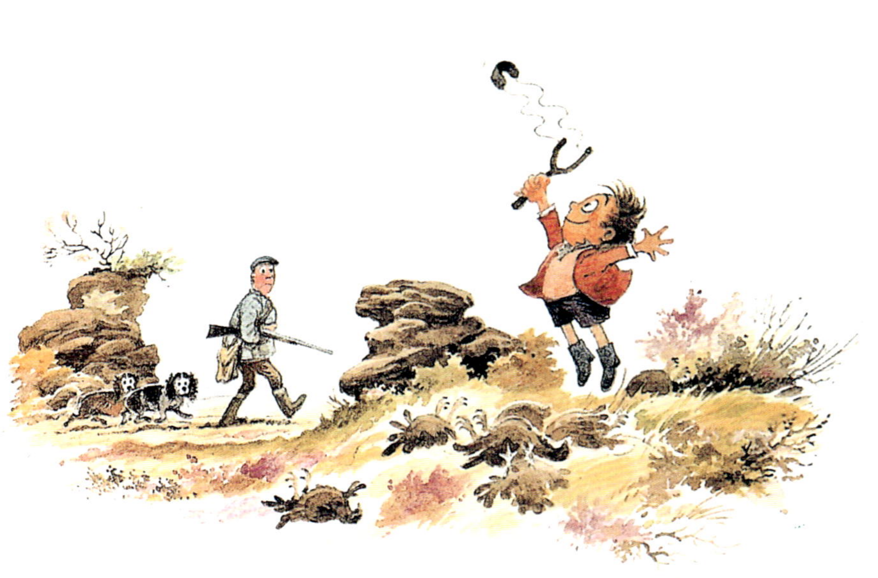

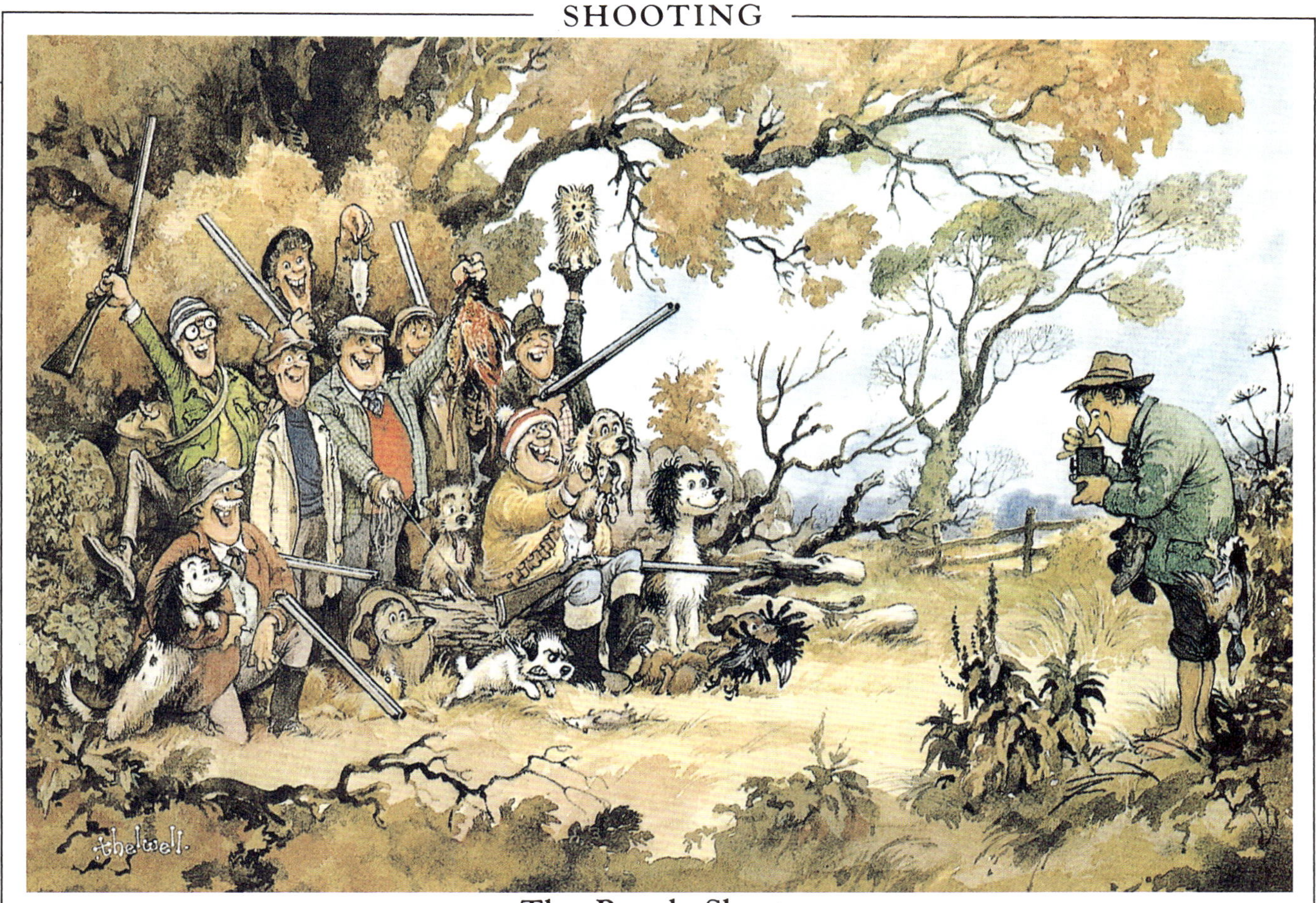

The Rough Shoot

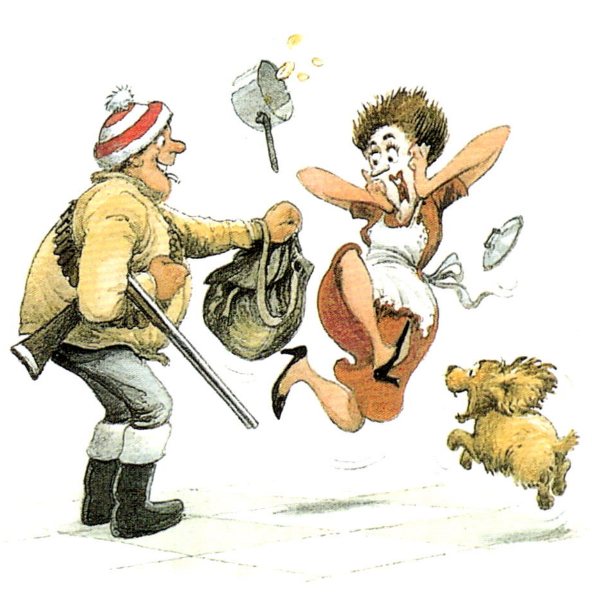

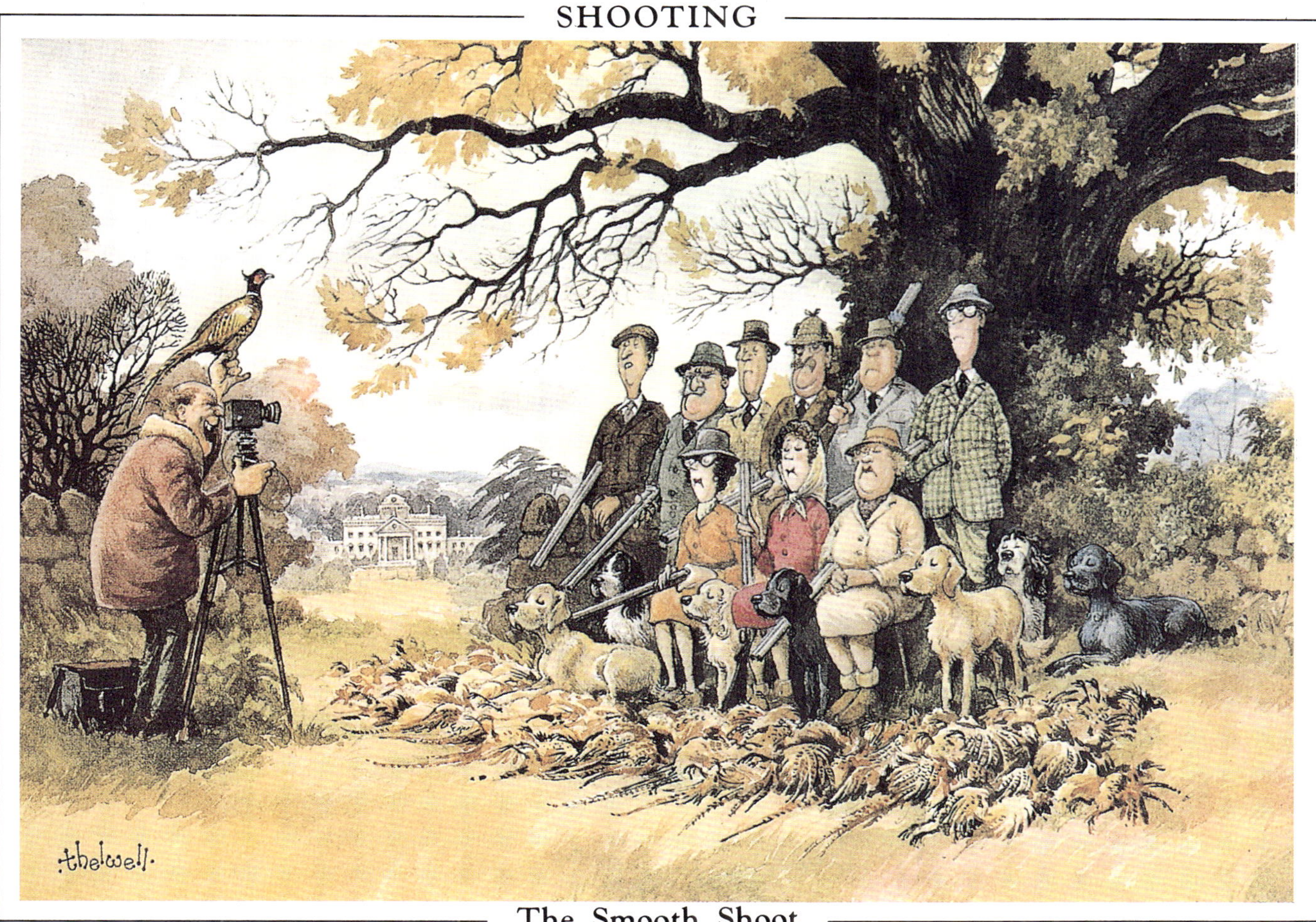

The Smooth Shoot

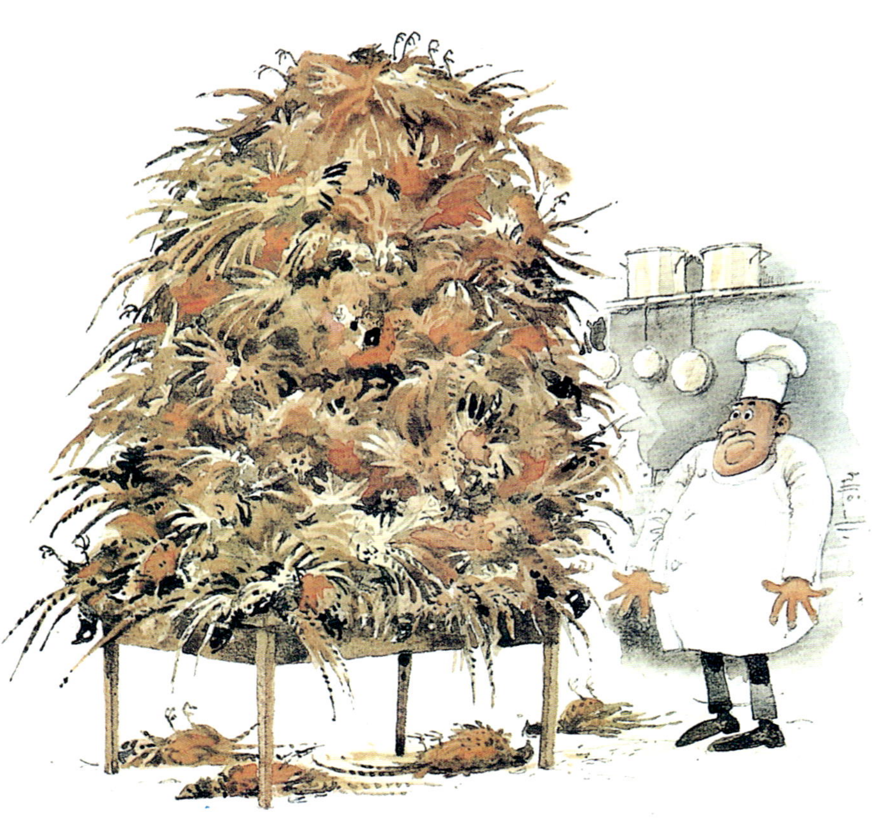

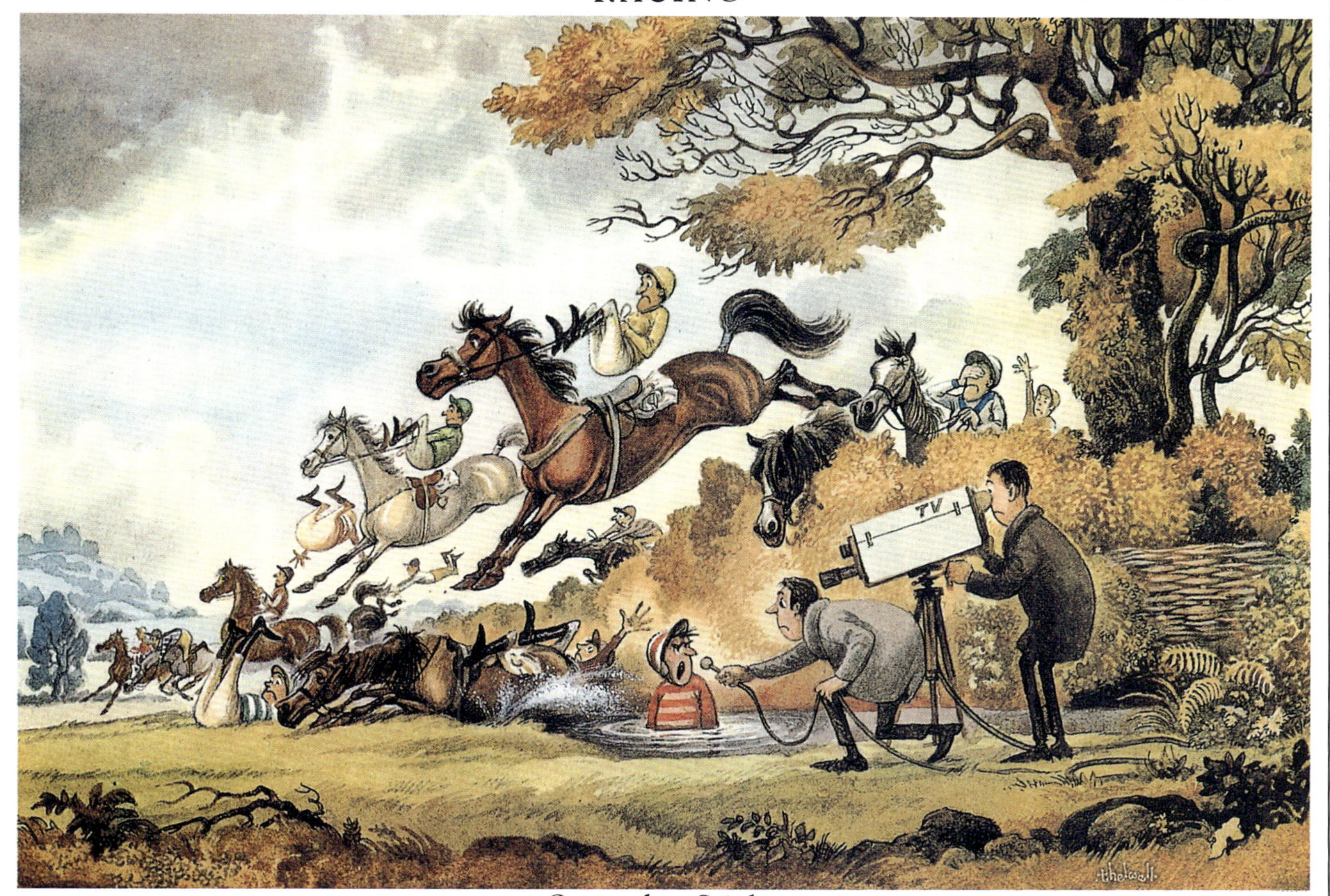

Over the Sticks

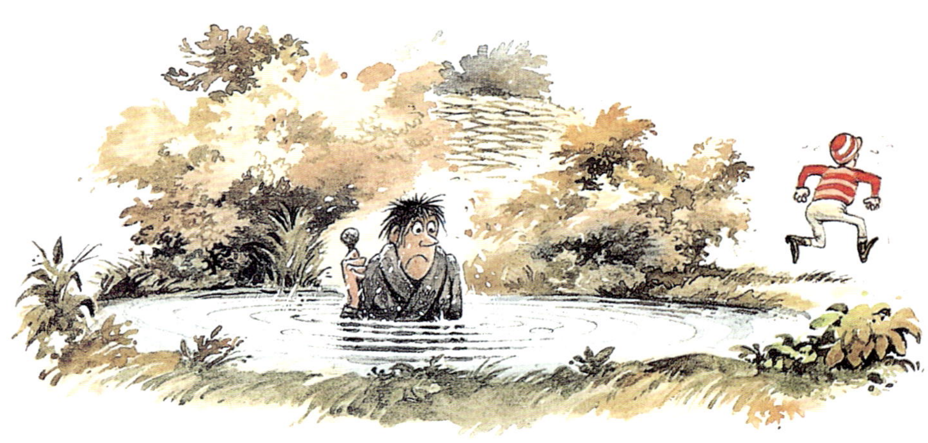

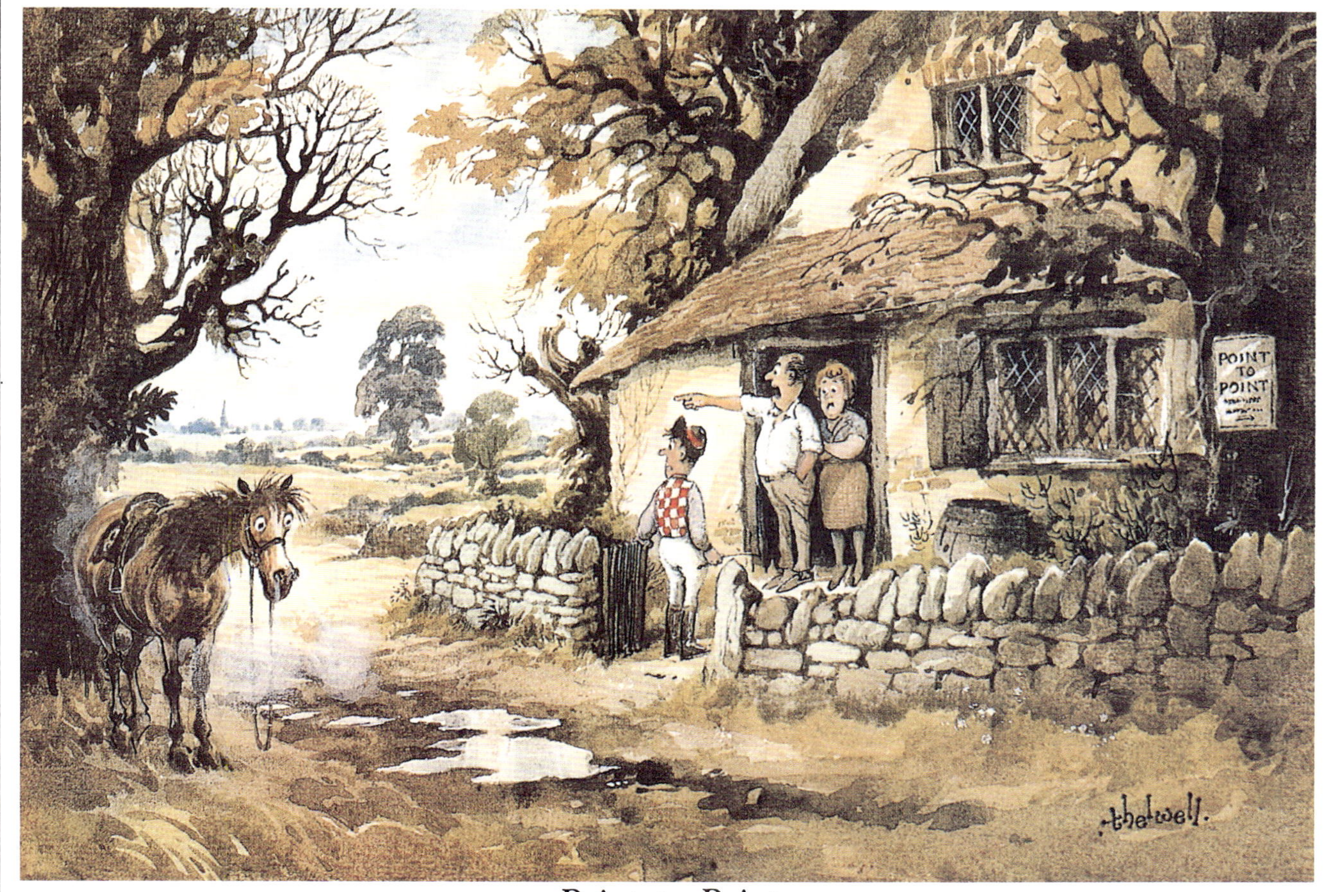

Point to Point

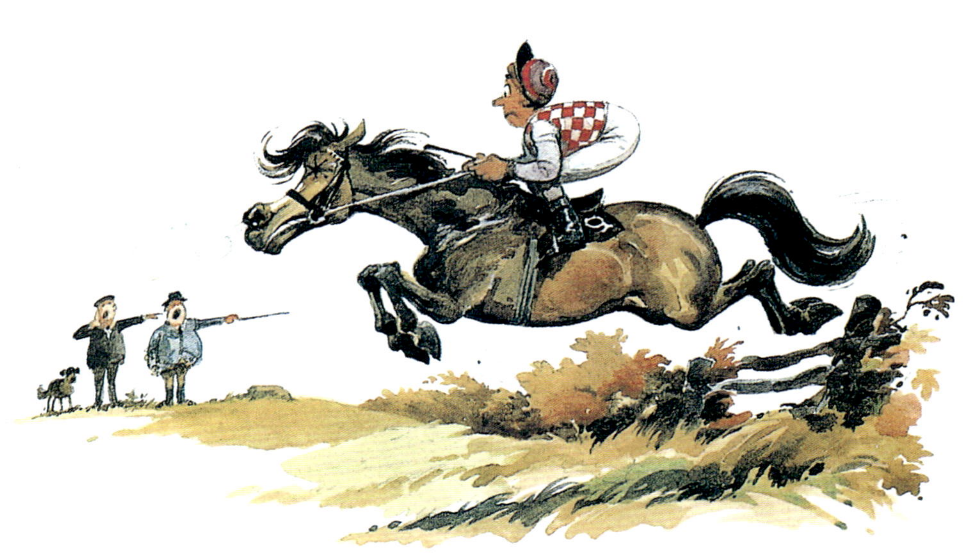

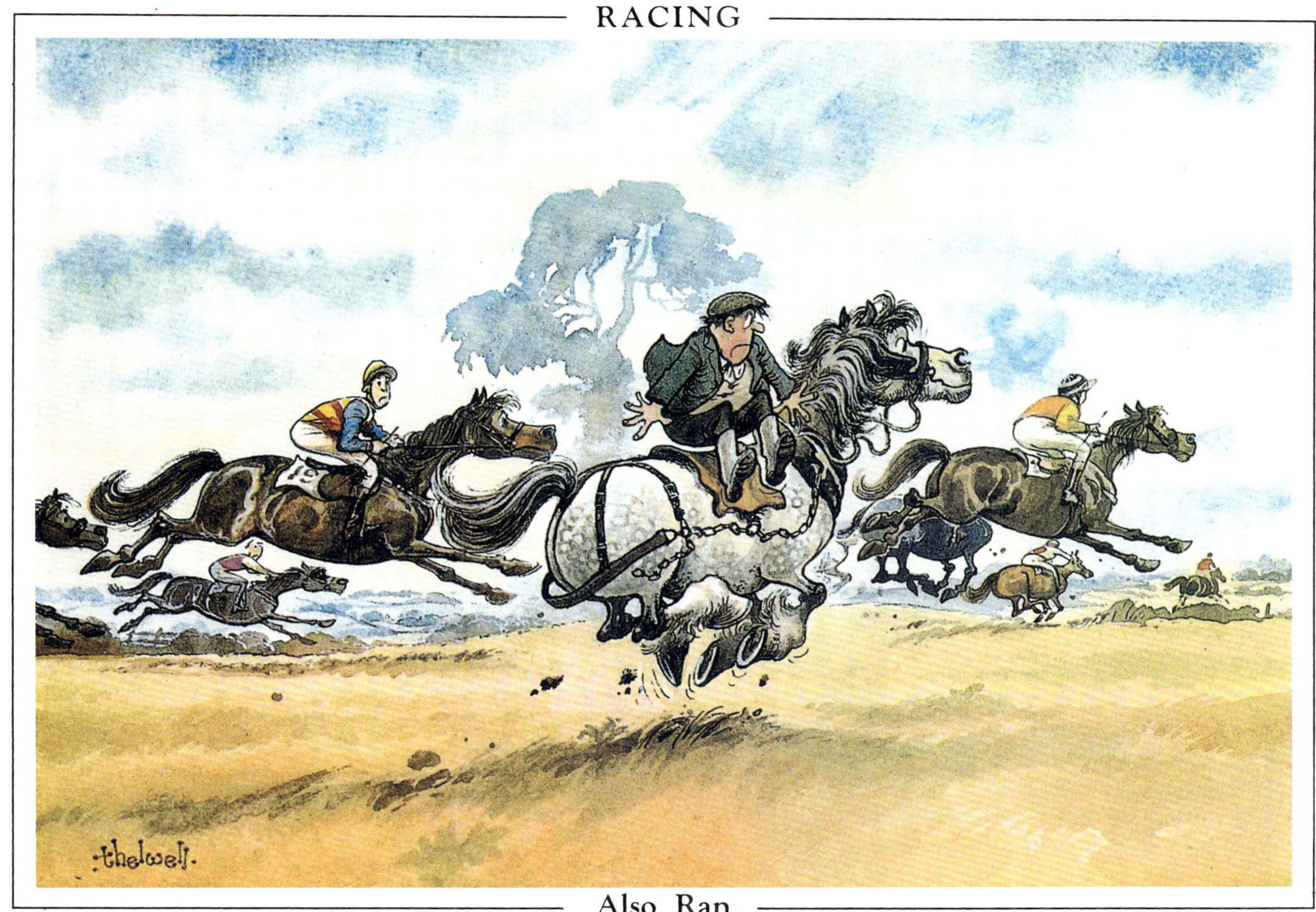

Also Ran

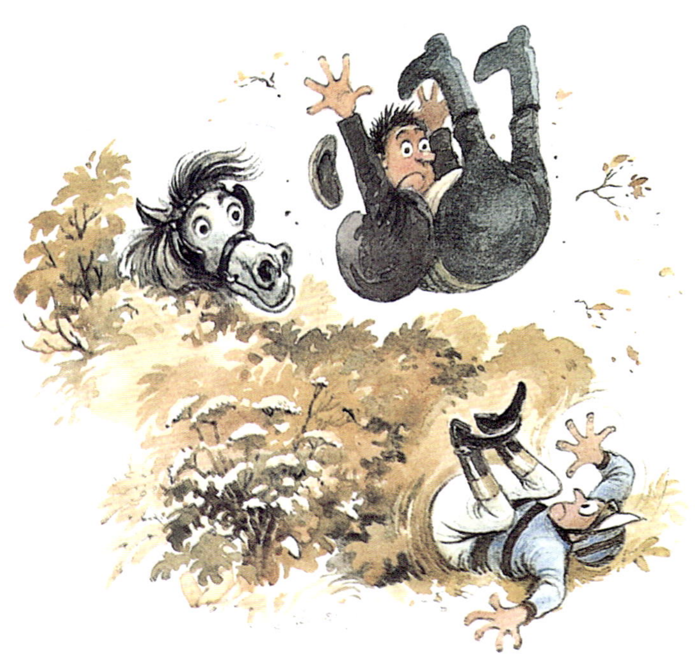

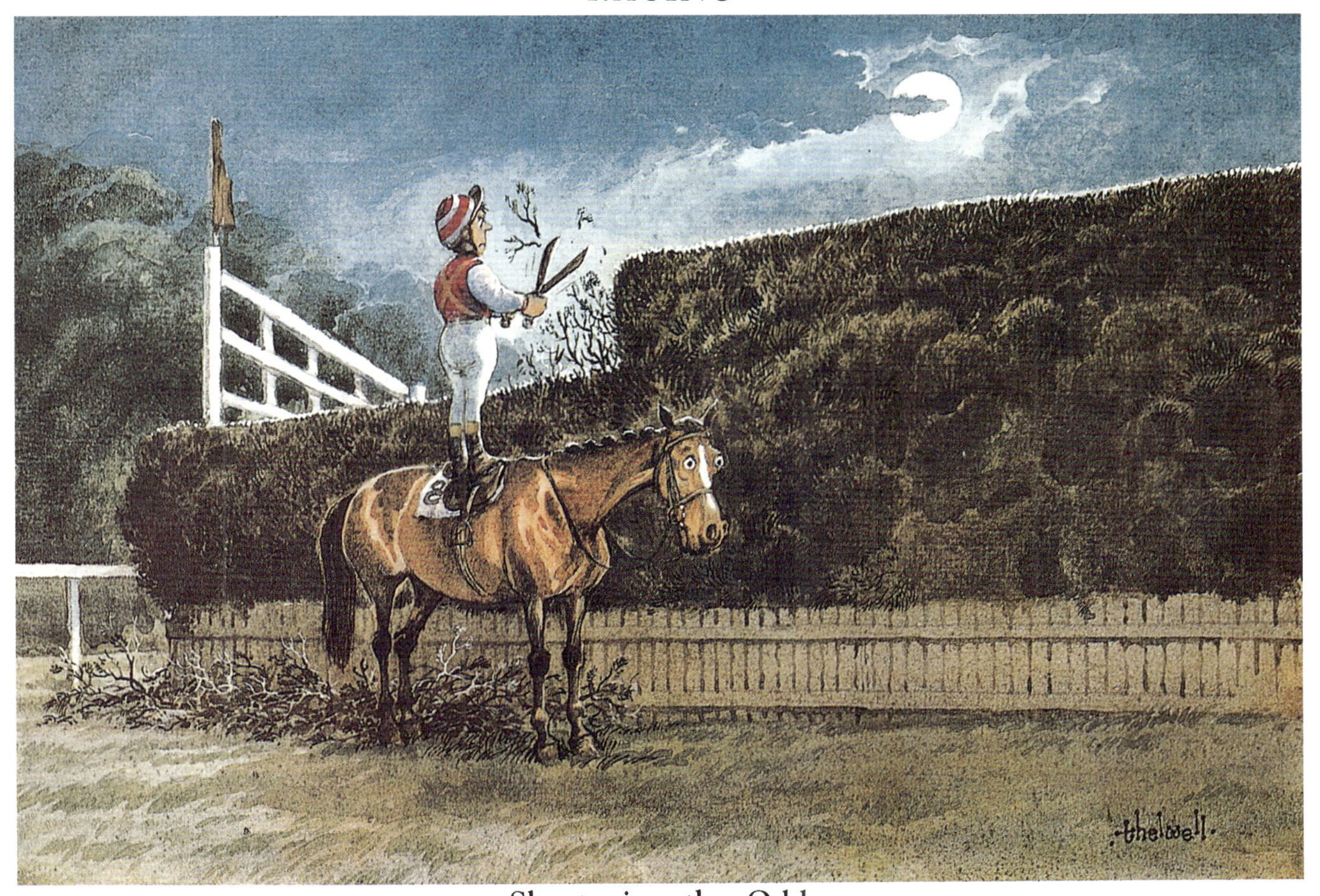

Shortening the Odds

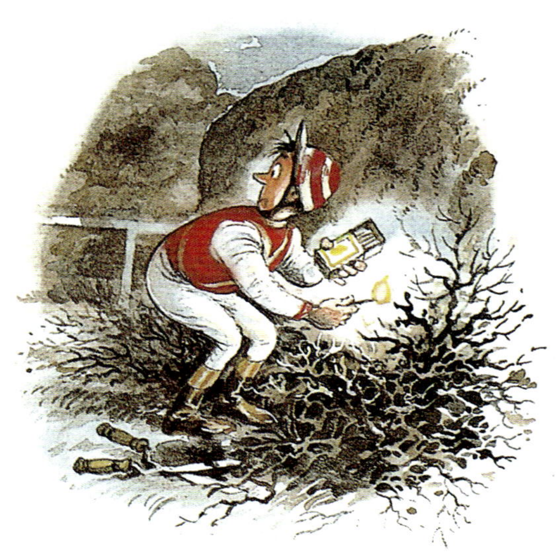

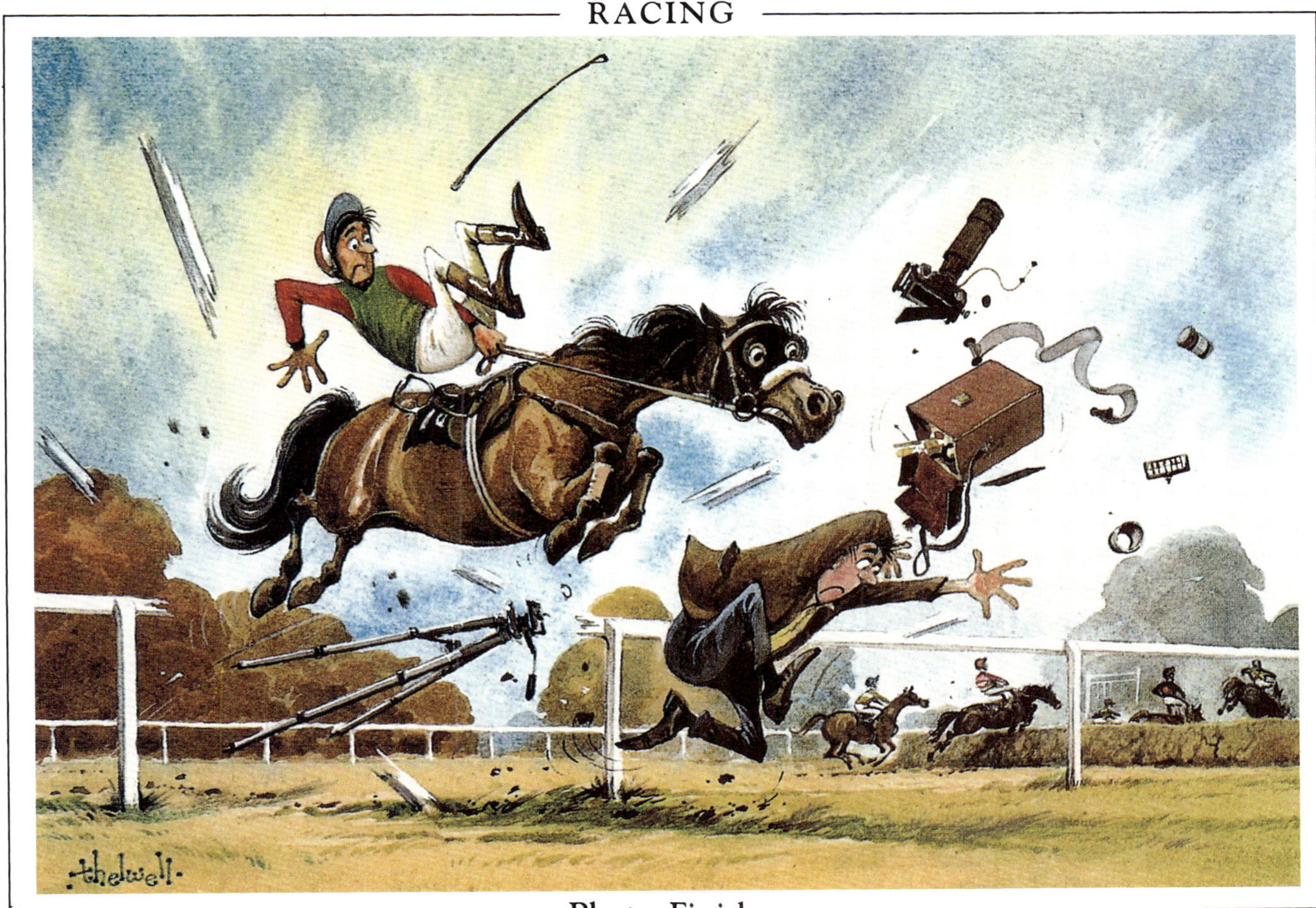

Photo Finish

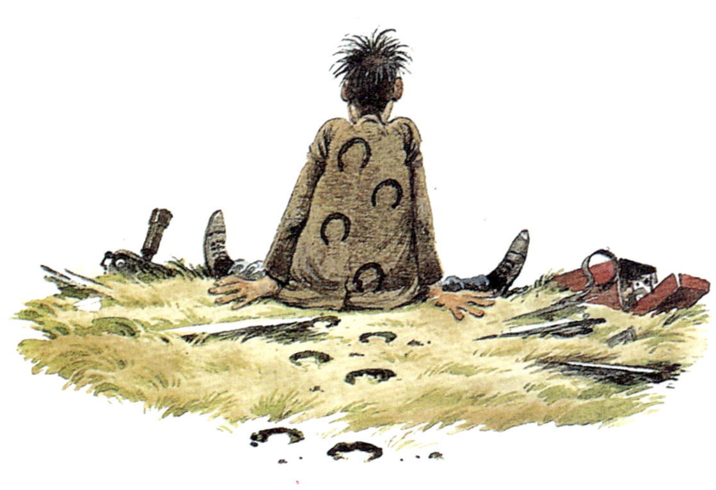

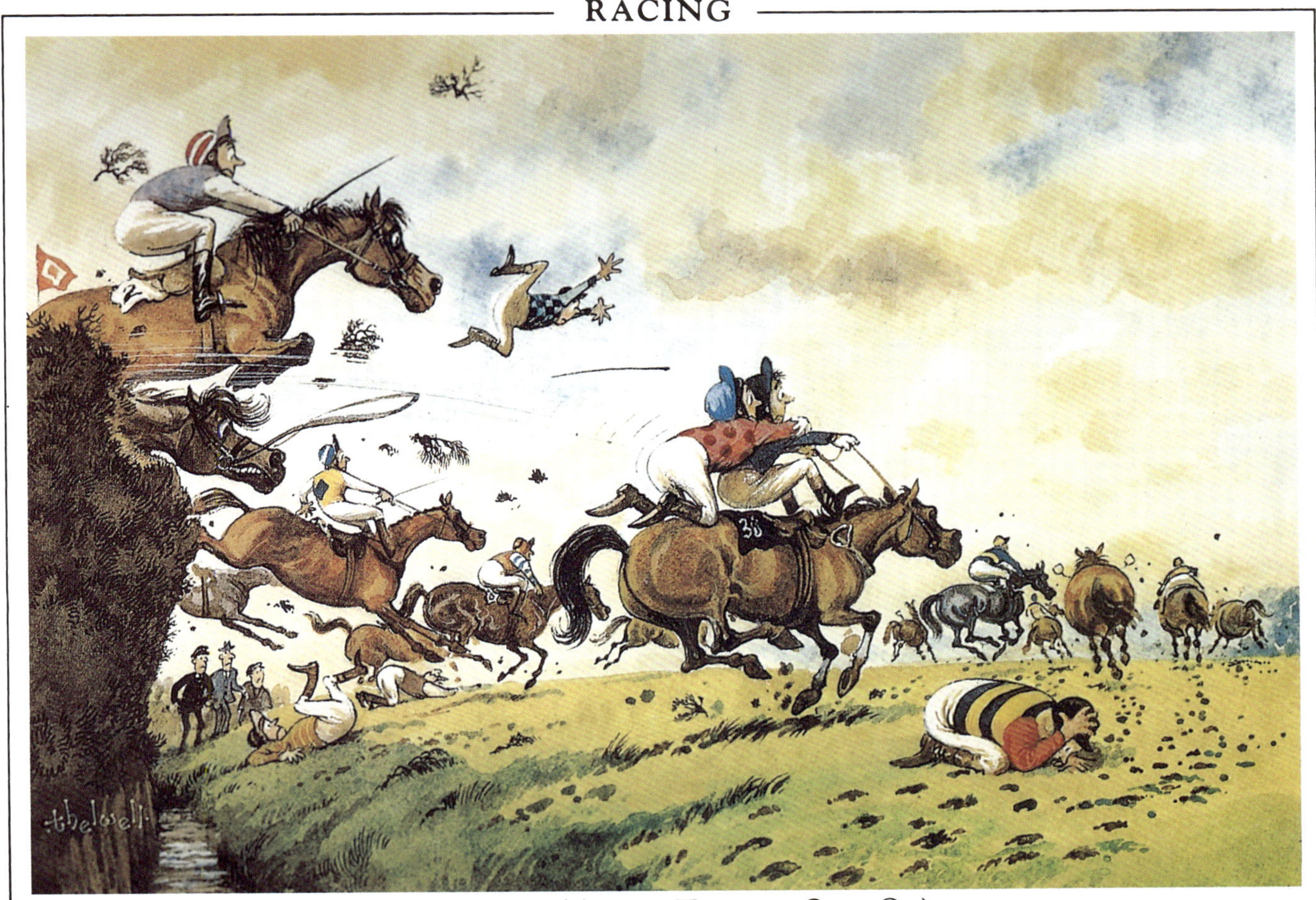

Tote Double (or Two to One On)

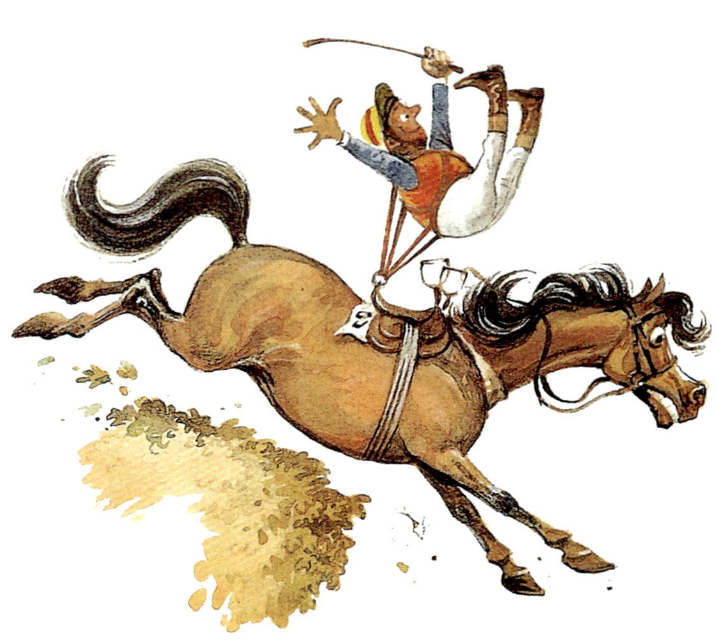

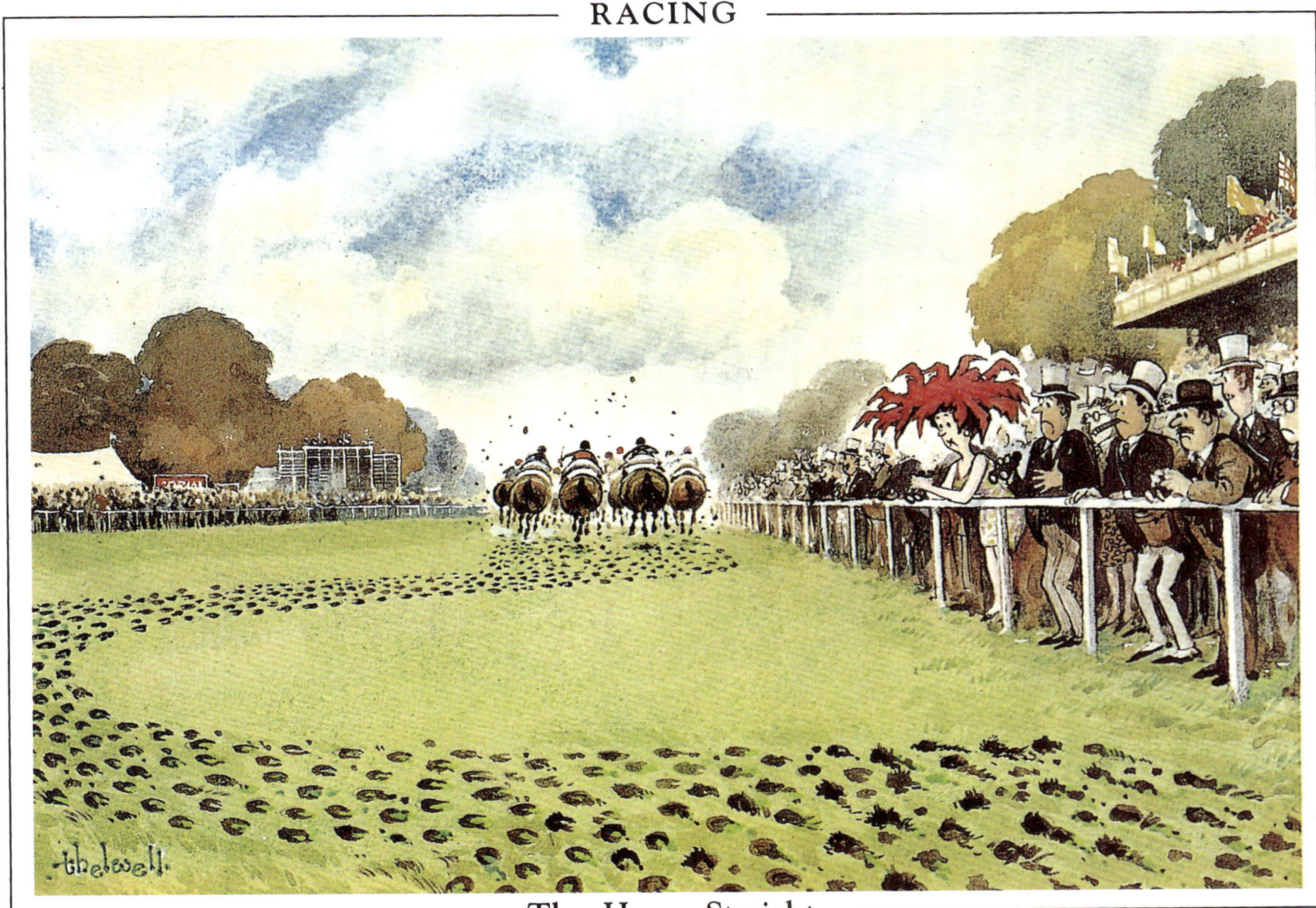

The Home Straight

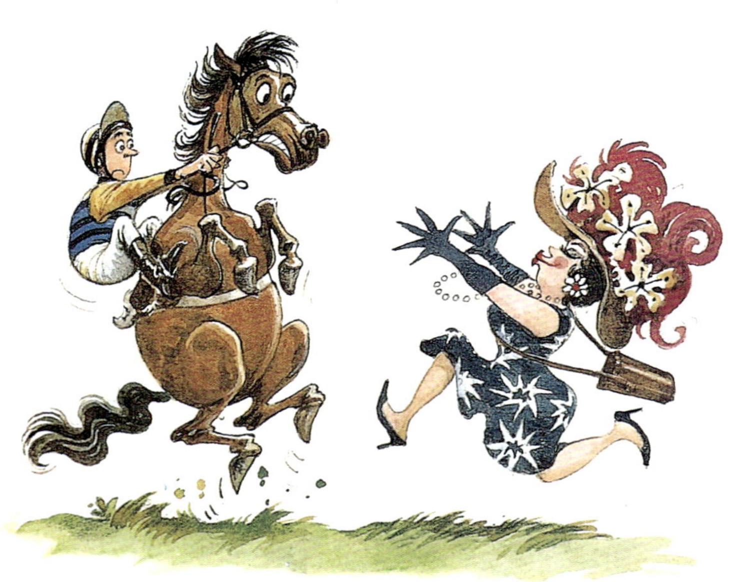